LOST GOLD
& BURIED
TREASURE

LOST GOLD & BURIED TREASURE

A Treasure Hunter's Guide to 100 Fortunes Waiting to Be Found

KEVIN D. RANDLE

M. EVANS AND COMPANY, INC.
New York

M. Evans and Company, Inc.
216 East 49th Street
New York, New York 10017

Library of Congress Cataloging-in-Publication Data

Randle, Kevin D., 1949–
    Lost gold & buried treasure : a treasure hunter's guide to 100
fortunes waiting to be found / Kevin D. Randle.
        p.   cm.
    Includes bibliographical references (p.   –   ) and index.
    ISBN 0-87131-792-3 (cl)
    1. Treasure-trove—United States.   I. Title.
G525.R295   1995
910.4′5—dc20   95-34592
                                                                      CIP

DESIGN BY BERNARD SCHLEIFER

Maps by Arlene Goldberg

Typeset by Classic Type, Inc.

Printed and bound by BookCrafters, Inc.

Manufactured in the United States of America
9   8   7   6   5   4   3   2   1

CONTENTS

—

PART IV: REAL CACHES OF
BURIED TREASURE

PART V: APPENDIX

LOST GOLD
& BURIED
TREASURE

INTRODUCTION

—

People spend money to buy lottery tickets, take trips to Las Vegas, wander the desert in search of gold, all to get instant wealth without having to work for it. Tales of lost mines and buried treasure have inspired thousands to give up jobs, families, and even their lives. Stories of lost treasure have been handed down from generation to generation, inspiring sons to follow fathers, wives to follow husbands, and daughters to follow mothers.

Some of the stories are myths based on opinion. Black Beard raided the Atlantic and when he was finally brought to justice, there was no sign of the booty that everyone believed he had stolen. He must have buried it somewhere. No one knew where, but everyone believed.

Other stories came from the Old West. A man named Adams stumbled out of southwestern New Mexico telling a tale of Apache Indians and a valley filled with gold. To prove it he had one small nugget that brought him more than $800. Others claimed to have seen the valley.

Such wealth is only just out of the grasp of those who search for it. It's over the next hill, around the next bend, or in the next valley. A little more time, a little more money, and it will be found.

These are the stories of some of the more famous, and the not so famous, lost mines and buried treasures. These stories have been carefully researched so that the myth is taken out and the facts put in. In some cases, the stories were found to be little more than elaborate cons; all the evidence is presented in those instances. Why waste time searching for a treasure that never existed in the first place?

It seems that the most likely of the treasures are not the ones worth millions of dollars, but those whose value is only a few thousands of dollars. Hundreds of these stashes have been buried and lost over the years. Gold coins hidden a hundred years ago are now worth thousands of dollars each to a collector. And finding a cache of fifty or a hundred thousand makes the months or years of searching well worth the effort.

So here are the stories of lost mines and buried treasures, with the myth taken out. Here are suggestions of where to look and what the payoff might be when found. But remember, most of the land is now private property and permission must be asked before the search can begin.

And remember also, in some cases people have been killed searching for treasure. There are those who jealously guard their secrets. Caution must be exercised.

Sit back and read these tales. And remember one other fact. Most tales of lost treasure are just like the lottery. Very few people will ever get rich searching for them. But if you don't look, then your chances of finding them are zero.

PART 1

TALES OF LOST MINES

1

THE LOST ADAMS

NEW MEXICO

FOR A TIME, IN THE MOVIES, IT was known as *MacKenna's Gold*, and for a short period in the last century some called it the Lost Baxter, but most know it under its original and most common name, the Lost Adams. For more than a century and a half people have searched for what would be the richest of the placer gold deposits ever found. And like all these stories, it begins with a massacre of the miners by the Apaches because of broken trusts and violations of agreements.

"It was the autumn of 1864," the man known now only as Adams would tell his audience. "I was returning to Los Angeles after running freight over to El Paso."

He always started the story the same way. A freight trip to El Paso and a rude awakening one morning as Apaches ran off his horses. He gave chase and recaptured the animals, but when he returned to his camp, he found his wagons burned. The Apaches had destroyed his camp and stolen his supplies. With only the horses he had saved, he decided to head for the nearby Pima Indian reservation where he could replace all that he had lost.

13

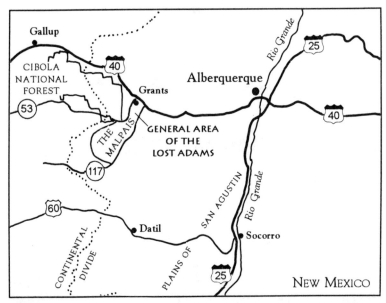

Arriving just before noon, he found a dozen or more prospectors there, excited about a minor gold strike close by. They were flashing small nuggets and making plans to return to the gold field. One of the Indians thought the excitement was funny because he knew where there was so much more gold; the scattered nuggets were the size of hen's eggs.

He told the group that he was really a Mexican, but that as a boy he had been captured by the Apaches, raised by them, and taught their traditions and their culture. While he lived with the Indians, they had taken him to a canyon filled with gold. "You can load a packhorse in a day," he boasted to them.

Of course none of the prospectors believed his story, but in the Pima village he had a reputation for honesty. The prospectors questioned him carefully and were eventually impressed by the answers he gave. He could describe, in detail, the area around the canyon, the trails leading to it, and what it looked like on the inside. The story didn't change even as the prospectors became more excited.

To prove his honesty, the Mexican told the prospectors he wanted no gold, just a horse and a rifle, to be given to him when he showed them the canyon. If he lied to them, if he failed to find the gold, then they could kill him. That offer seemed to convince the most skeptical of the prospectors.

Adams arrived as the prospecting party was preparing to leave. Since Adams knew several of the prospectors, they invited him to accompany them.

Those who heard the story from Adams said he would grin at this point and say, "As I had nothing else in sight, I joined the company."

Adams later provided a set of general directions for those who would follow in his footsteps. From the Pima village the prospectors headed to the northeast until they reached the Continental Divide. They worked their way down to an open plain and continued for another fifteen miles or so. Then, without having seen any prominent landmarks, not even a trail, they turned due north. In the distance was a long range of mountains and keeping it in sight, they traveled another six or seven miles.

Stopping suddenly, the Mexican pointed to a faint wagon trail and cautioned the men, "Mark this spot well. You will have to come back to this point. Turn east to find Fort Wingate. Remember this spot well."

They continued for several miles, moving in a northerly direction, and then dropped down into a deep canyon. They followed it for several miles, winding back and forth until the trail widened out onto a small plateau about five hundred feet above the surrounding territory.

The plateau had been cultivated by Indians. The prospectors found remains of corn, beans, and a patch of pumpkins. The pumpkins would later figurer in the legend that grew up around the Lost Adams.

On the other side of the plateau they entered an arroyo, followed the dry creek bed, and then a zigzag path through the cliffs. They came to a narrow passage and entered another arroyo. They zigzagged upward about a thousand feet and then stopped.

Their guide pointed and said, "In the distance are two rounded mountains. The gold is in a canyon at the foot of those peaks. We'll be there tomorrow."

But just ahead of them was a beautiful, tree-lined, grass-covered valley with a stream through the center. At the far end was a waterfall. The prospectors led their horses to the water and as the animals began to drink, the miners noticed the first of the nuggets. Dozens of them sparkled in the stream bed. Hundreds were lying mixed with the sand along the bank. Gold seemed to be everywhere. They had yet to reach the main canyon of gold.

One man jumped into the stream, reached down, and found a huge nugget. Another was filling his pockets as fast as he could. Still others were laughing or slapping each other on the back. They had found more gold than any one of them had imagined he would ever see in one location in his life and it was just laying around waiting to be taken.

When they settled down, they told the Mexican that they were satisfied. He had more than fulfilled his promise. They were going to stay where they were because of the trees, the stream, and game. Plenty of gold was available and they didn't need to see the bigger vein at the far end of the canyon. They paid the Mexican the horse and rifle they had promised and he disappeared immediately.

That night, sitting around the campfire, they began to plan seriously. There was so much gold that they could spend years gathering it and still have tons of it left. They decided that they would all share in it equally, but not all would do the mining. They would need more supplies. One group would go for them. Another party would build a camp so they would have some shelter. The third, the largest of the parties, would mine the gold.

All agreed except for a German, Emil Schaeffer. He was afraid of the Apaches and asked to be left out. He would gather all that he needed and then get out as quickly as he could. He didn't want to be killed.

With the gold so easily available, they felt no pressure. They spent the first full day exploring the stream that meandered through the long, box canyon. A small party cut down some trees to begin building the camp. Only a few of them did any real prospecting, except for Schaeffer. He stayed to himself, gathering nuggets and loading his packhorse.

The next day a party left for provisions. They planned to use a few of the nuggets to pay for the supplies. Schaeffer said he would accompany them. Adams believed that Schaeffer left with about $13,000 in gold. Schaeffer abandoned the provisioning party at Fort Wingate.

The Apaches did find the miners as Schaeffer had feared, but didn't attack. They warned the prospectors not to venture above the falls at the far end of the canyon. If the prospectors remained where they were, they could take all the gold they could carry away.

That inspired a couple of the men. They remembered what the Mexican had said and wondered what was above the falls. Although they hadn't been interested the first couple of days, now they wanted to see what was hidden there. They didn't think it would hurt for them to take a look. They returned with tales of the "mother lode." If they thought the nuggets were big where they were, they told their fellows, they should see what was scattered above the falls. The nuggets were twice, three times as large as those they were collecting. One of the men showed a nugget he had picked up.

THE APACHES ATTACK

Eight days after the provisioning party left, they were expected to return but didn't. On the ninth day, Adams and his bunkmate, Dutch Davis, decided to ride out to meet them. As they neared the entrance to the canyon, they heard shooting. They crept closer and found that the Apaches had attacked the provisioning party. By the time Adams and Davis got close enough to see, all those in the provisioning party were dead, the supplies scattered.

Adams knew that they had to warn the others. He raced back along the arroyo with Davis but before they could arrive, the miners there had been attacked as well. Concealing themselves among the rocks, trees, and bushes high on the side of the arroyo, they watched the attack by the Apaches.

Three prospectors were trapped in the open on the banks of the stream. They were fighting for their lives, but being killed rapidly. One man broke from the defense and tried to reach the cabin but the Apaches caught and killed him.

Now the only survivors, other than Adams and Davis, were the men in the cabin. The Indians set the cabin on fire and waited for the miners to flee. As they left their cover, the Apaches killed them.

Adams knew that there was nothing he could do to help his friends. His only chance for survival was to remain, with Davis, concealed among the rocks. He could hear the Apaches below celebrating their victory.

In later years Adams would describe the horror that he had seen after the massacre. The Apaches who had killed the provisioning party joined those who attacked the cabin. Adams saw the heads of some of the miners on stakes. The Indians cut the arms and legs off the bodies of the dead prospectors and danced around the bodies in celebration, waving the grisly trophies.

Adams knew the Apaches weren't stupid. They had been watching the prospectors for days and would soon discover that two men had escaped. The only chance he and Davis had for survival was to wait for dark and then get out of the canyon without any of the gold.

They remained where they were through the heat of the afternoon. Adams was tempted to try to sneak down to the stream for water but decided that it was too risky. Although the Apaches had disappeared, he was sure that one had been left behind, hidden, in case the two missing miners tried to reach the cabin.

Adams was also thinking of the coffee pot full of gold nuggets that had been concealed beneath the rocks used for a hearth in the cabin. Adams would later estimate that more than a hundred thousand dollars in gold had been hidden during the few days they had actively prospected. He stayed concealed throughout the afternoon, watching the smoldering remains and searching for signs that the Apaches were near.

Even after nightfall Adams and Davis remained hidden for a while longer. It was about midnight when thirst finally forced them from hiding. Later Adams would tell audiences, "The first thing we did was to make our way back to the log cabin. I thought we might be able to get the gold hidden there." But the fire wasn't out and the embers were still smoldering. It was too hot to get anywhere near the hearth and the gold buried under it.

They were filling their canteens in the stream when Adams remembered two nuggets he had hidden by a tree stump on the first day of prospecting. Those he could recover with little effort and no additional danger.

They escaped from the canyon, leaving the remains of their dead fellows behind them. They worked their way along the zigzag canyon, climbed down to the plateau with the pumpkin patch, and crossed it. By then the eastern sky was beginning to lighten and Adams didn't want to travel during the day. Before hiding, they tried to wipe out signs they had been present, using brush to obscure their footprints.

With the first light came the first of the Apache scouts searching for them. Although the Indians passed close to their hiding place once or twice, they didn't find it. Late in the afternoon, another group passed by, but they too failed to find the hiding men.

That night Adams and Davis left the plateau, navigated the last zigzag canyon, followed the dry stream bed, and finally emerged into the open desert. By morning they had left the canyon miles behind and decided to keep going. Adams was convinced they had fooled the Apaches. Now it was important to reach civilization quickly. They traveled through the day and by nightfall had finished the last of their water.

For the next seven days they traveled, resting through the heat of the afternoon. They ate wild grass, acorns, and weeds, and found enough water to keep alive. Twice they dodged Apache search parties and on the seventh day they spotted a third. By now, according to Adams, they were too tired, hungry, and discouraged to care. They continued to travel, and the Indians they met along the way were friendly. At the end of the seventh day, Adams and Davis entered the friendly camp.

Adams remained with the Indians for weeks to regain his health. When he felt better, he returned to Los Angeles where he told his story to many and provided his listeners with maps, but didn't try to return to New Mexico himself. Not long after his return to L.A., he contracted typhoid fever and it took him months to recover.

In a slightly different version of the story, Adams and his friend, now named Davidson, stumbled through the New Mexican desert for a number of days. When their horses dropped, exhausted, the men shot them and boiled the meat for something to eat. They walked until the soles of their boots wore out and then threw them away. They found the wagon track that would take them back to Fort Wingate, but Adams didn't know in which direction to turn. Apparently he picked the wrong one. One day they spotted horsemen in the distance but no longer cared whether they were Apaches or not. As the men approached, Adams saw that it was a roving cavalry patrol from Fort Apache.

After recuperating, Adams showed the Army doctor at Fort Apache one of the nuggets he had saved. Adams shared with him all the information he had about the canyon and the landmarks. The doctor said that he thought he might try to find the gold himself someday.

ADAMS AND THE SEARCHERS FOR THE CANYON OF GOLD

Adams did return to New Mexico many times. The first time he didn't begin at the Pima village, believing that he could find the gold by starting the search closer to the canyon. Adams said, "I thought I could go more direct to the spot if I entered from a nearer cut many miles north of the Pima village, but I could not get on the right trail."

Adams continued to search for the lost canyon of gold until his death. He took out many different parties, sometimes starting at the Pima village, sometimes at different locations. He tried to find the wagon trail, the pumpkin patch, and the two rounded mountains, but always failed.

Those who traveled with him, paying for the expeditions, believed Adams to be an honest man. C.A. Shaw, a retired sea captain, accompanied Adams and heard his story many times. Shaw said that he listened to Adams over a period of two years and Adams' story was always the same. Shaw was convinced that Adams was telling the truth about the canyon and the gold.

In 1874 Shaw financed the first of the trips into New Mexico. For days Adams led Shaw and a party of fourteen men in circles in western New Mexico. Adams wasn't sure what river they had crossed during the original expedition, and then wasn't sure if they hadn't crossed two rivers. Adams changed his mind once too often for those with him and the expedition fell apart. One group thought that Adams was a liar and should be shot as a fraud. The other, led by Shaw, was convinced that Adams was telling the truth and would lead them to vast riches. After all, said Shaw, it had been ten years since Adams had seen the canyon and the New Mexican landscape changed radically from season to season.

Two years later, in 1876, Adams and Shaw were back in New Mexico. For two months they circled western New Mexico, unable to find the landmarks Adams had seen more than a decade before. In Reserve, New Mexico, after several hours of drinking at a local saloon, some of the party decided that Adams was lying. If he wouldn't lead them to the gold immediately, they were going to hang him. Fortunately for Adams, another man, Wash Jones, who had searched for the gold himself, and who knew the tale, got Adams out of the saloon and took him to Socorro.

In Socorro, Adams was the house guest of Robert Lewis. For years Lewis had looked for the Lost Adams and now the man of the legend was staying at his house. That was apparently the end of the 1876 Adams expedition.

OTHERS TAKE OVER THE SEARCH

After Adams died, about 1886, Shaw organized his own expeditions, starting in the Pima villages in southwestern Arizona. Five days' travel to the northwest would bring them to the mountains of the Continental Divide. Shaw believed that the Lost Adams was in Socorro County, New Mexico, and was often seen in Socorro buying supplies.

But Shaw claimed he had found other corroboration for the Lost Adams. On one of his trips, he left Los Angeles and headed straight for Fort Wingate in northwestern New Mexico. There he found the same officer in charge who was in command when the nine men from the original expedition arrived to buy their supplies. The officer told Shaw that the men had come in late one evening, rushed around, and were considerably excited. They told the officer they had left their fellows working a wonderfully rich gold mine and were in a hurry to return to it.

Interestingly, the nine men weren't at all reluctant to give general directions to the mine. The story as told by the officer provided instructions as to distances and the time it took to reach the gold field in the Zuni Mountains. According to the officer, a prospector needed to travel north or northeast from the malpais (lava beds) about fifty miles. There was an old wagon road from Fort Wingate and from that point in the malpais the road led ten miles to the west. There was a deep canyon that led off to the north for five miles to a mesa, across the mesa (the plateau with the pumpkin patch) to a canyon nearby. It zigzagged back and forth for another five miles and narrowed to a point where a single man on horseback could ride through only by scraping against the sides of the pass. Beyond was 14 Mile Canyon, at the head of which was the place the Lost Adams was found.

That satisfied Shaw, once and for all, that the Lost Adams existed. He'd traveled with Adams, he'd stomped over west-central New Mexico near Socorro, and now he had heard the story told by the officer at Fort Wingate. He was convinced. Before Shaw died in 1917, he shared his research with W.H. Byerts of Socorro. Together, with Byerts supplying financing and Shaw providing his knowledge based on what Adams and the Fort Wingate officer told him, they searched for the gold. Byerts also claimed to have heard other first-hand accounts, including those told by Dick Patterson, and several others.

In 1881 the Fort Apache doctor appeared in Socorro. Those accompanying him were not tough and the doctor knew that he wouldn't survive with just these men. In Socorro he was directed to Bob Dowling who was organizing his own party to search for the gold. The doctor volunteered to help finance the whole expedition on the condition that one of his men accompany Dowling and his group to watch out for his interests.

Dowling claimed that his party did find the canyon. They rode up a dry stream bed and came to a place where the stream would have plunged over a waterfall, if there had been any water. They didn't find the ruins of a cabin but did find an area where trees had been cut down many years earlier. They explored the area for hours but found no gold at all. His story, at odds with most of the others, could provide the one clue that explains the fate of the Lost Adams.

After returning empty-handed to Socorro, Dowling wrote to the doctor explaining the situation. With that, both men stopped searching for the Lost Adams, believing that Dowling had found the correct location.

Others told of similar stories. A rancher living along the Frisco River in western Socorro County told of a band of thirty Mexicans arriving at his ranch in search of the Lost Adams. They had an excess of baggage and asked the rancher to store some of it for them. He agreed and watched as they left, led by a half-Mexican and half-Indian guide, heading off into the malpais. A few weeks later they returned, seemed to be happy, and paid for the storage of their baggage. They said they would be back the next year.

About a year later the band was back. The rancher believed it was the same group. They again asked to store the excess baggage. They explained they had found and were working an extremely rich mine. The rancher asked to go with them, but the Mexicans refused. They said they would allow him to go with them the next time. But they never returned. All the rancher knew was that they headed off in the same direction and he believed they were working the Lost Adams.

THE LOST BAXTER

Two more men claimed to have found the canyon of gold. Jason Baxter and John Aldair spent months searching for the Lost Adams but found nothing of interest. Finally they headed into the Datil Mountains north of the Plains of San Agustin. They spent weeks searching but finally ran out of water. One night a thirsty mule broke loose. Baxter let it go, hoping that it would lead them to water.

The mule headed straight for a lone mountain, climbed one slope, and then followed a ridge. It dipped into a canyon that switched back and forth, left that canyon, and then disappeared into the side of a cliff. When Baxter reached the rocky wall, he found a narrow passage through it.

Baxter told Aldair about what he had found and then worked his way through until he came out on a grass-covered mesa.

Across the flat ground, standing at the base of another cliff, was the mule. Before Baxter could take a step, the mule disappeared again and Baxter followed it through that opening, too. Baxter and Aldair found their mule pawing at the soft sand, which quickly filled with water.

Baxter was worried about Indians finding them. Here was an oasis in the middle of high desert and Baxter knew that every Indian in the region would know of it. Against the cliff, under an overhang, he built a short, semicircular rock wall to offer some protection and concealment in case hostile Indians found them.

Hidden behind the short rock wall, they cooked dinner, kicked out the fire, and then went to sleep. About two o'clock the following morning both men began to get jumpy. The pack animals were pawing at the ground. Just before dawn a wild turkey began to gobble. It was answered by several others.

As the sun came up, an arrow flashed by. Trapped against the cliff, in a long, narrow box canyon where there was little chance of rescue by a roving cavalry patrol, their options were extremely limited. They couldn't run for it because there was too much open ground. Then, late in the afternoon, Aldair caught an arrow in the foot.

Near sundown a summer storm began to brew. Entering the canyon, Baxter had noticed driftwood caught high on the canyon walls. In the southwest, flash floods were a real danger. Experienced men never camped in arroyos or along flood plains, knowing that rain fifty miles away could fill the canyons around them with water in a matter of minutes. Too many men had been killed by the unexpected high water.

With darkness came the storm. In the slashing rain and under the cover of darkness, Baxter and Aldair began to work their way deeper into the canyon. In the distance they could hear the Indians trying to follow them.

Aldair's wound was making it difficult for them to travel. With the rain coming down harder each minute, Aldair wanted Baxter to leave him and get out, but Baxter refused. They continued to move deeper into the canyon, hoping to find a way to higher ground and escape.

They entered a narrow passage that opened into a small valley. As the lightning stroked, they could see, in the light of the brief flashes, a small stream and the ruins of an old log cabin. Baxter noticed an old sluice box near the cabin; scattered around the box and the cabin were bones. Among those bones was a human skull.

There wasn't time for Baxter to search the area for additional clues. The Apaches were getting closer and the weather wasn't improving. Baxter and Aldair continued to move toward and then above the falls. In the darkness and rain, they eluded the Apaches and escaped from the valley, climbing the steep rock walls.

But Baxter knew what he had seen and was sure that he had finally found the Lost Adams. All the clues were there: the ruined cabin, the green valley, and even the skeletal remains of the massacred miners.

It was eight years before Baxter was able to return. Unlike Adams, he was able to remember the path he had followed into the area and the one he had used to escape from it. He remembered the hidden mesa, found it, and crossed it. Everything was there as he remembered.

Then he entered the first valley. It was not as he remembered it. Gone were the trees, water, and animals. It looked as if something had swept it clean. The entrance to the valley was choked with debris. In the narrow passage were huge boulders, broken trees, and torn up bushes. All traces of the stream were gone. Without the readily available water, Baxter couldn't stay, but he planned to return with the proper equipment. He never made it.

MORE CORROBORATION
FOR THE LOST ADAMS

But the results of Baxter's search didn't discourage many of the others. They still argued about the Adams tale. One man, called "Doc" Young, approached it from another angle. He remembered Adams talking of a German who had left the canyon with the provisioning party. Young traced the German, Schaeffer, to Europe and found him. Schaeffer, according to Young, told the same story as Adams. Schaeffer told Young all he could about the landmarks, the location, and the Apaches, but claimed he was too old and too sick to return to New Mexico. Young, now completely convinced the story was true, searched frequently, but never found the gold.

There are others who believe they did find the Lost Adams. An El Paso man, W.T. Tolbert, told reporters in 1918 he had bought a ranch just south of the malpais where he met a man named Johnson who claimed intimate knowledge of the Lost Adams. In fact, Johnson had originally heard the tale from Adams himself.

W.T. Tolbert said that while he lived on the ranch, several men came by searching for the Lost Adams. "Most were secretive, thinking they had the secret to the plot that would lead them to the gold," Tolbert said. "Some looked for an old crooked pine tree that they believed would point them to the canyon while others would be looking for two high, round mountains and an old trail running to the south of them . . ."

Tolbert said that he had watched dozens of prospectors come and go. The Lost Adams, according to all who searched for them, would be difficult to find. The Apaches had disguised the area, covered it, and then stopped paying merchants for supplies with gold nuggets. They didn't want the white men to know about or search for the location.

Adams himself had told everyone who would listen that a prospector or geologist would never find the gold. The country through which they had passed was old lava beds. From a distance, the landscape didn't appear to be very rough, but the deeper into it he traveled, the rougher and more broken it became. Adams said that the land didn't look as if it contained any gold at all.

But others did see the gold, including one archaeologist. Alvin D. Hudson reported that the archaeologist, a friend of his, was interested in Indian ruins and had been told there was a cliff dwelling in the malpais west of Albuquerque that had not been explored by other scientists. A man, who claimed he could take the archaeologist to the ruins, said that no white man had ever seen them. The ruins were visible only during the early morning when the sunlight was just right. The rest of the day they were hidden in the shadows of the cliff and if the archaeologist didn't know where to look, he'd never spot them.

There was a catch, however. The guide made it clear that he would take the archaeologist in to see the ruins but only the ruins. They could not look for gold. Until he was convinced that the archaeologist had no interest in gold, the guide wouldn't show him anything.

The guide made it clear that they would be watched while they were in the canyon. Once inside, the guide took the archaeologist to a spot where they could see the cliff dwelling. Standing there on the canyon floor, the guide told the archaeologist that there were a number of gold nuggets near his feet. Crouching casually, he picked up a handful of stones and began tossing them away. The archaeologist followed his lead and grabbed the nuggets as well as other stones. He flipped away all the rocks except a couple of the nuggets.

A day later, the two men left the canyon and returned to their car. The two small nuggets contained a great deal of gold, but the archaeologist was more interested in the cliff dwellings. At that time, around 1920, the rumors were that the Lost Adams was being guarded by Indians and outlaws. Anyone who approached too closely or entered the canyon would be killed.

MORE CORROBORATION

As late as 1927, Hudson, who had lived in El Paso for decades, was telling many stories about the Lost Adams. Interviewed by newspaper reporters, he said that growing up in Iowa in the 1880s, he had heard stories about the Lost Adams and its gold from those who had either seen or searched for the mine themselves. Hudson, in fact, believed that his uncles, Frank and Will Lee, had once seen the valley and the gold.

The Lee boys had headed west with other prospectors from Iowa and Missouri. They searched western New Mexico, finally making their way to the malpais. According to Hudson, after four years, everyone had given up. The Lee boys then found a 19-year-old black guide and the three of them found the Lost Adams gold.

According to the July 16, 1927 edition of the *El Paso Herald*, the guide had been located and interviewed, but it isn't clear if the reporter talked to him personally or not. The guide confirmed that they had found the Lost Adams in 1881, but they were attacked by Apaches while trying to get out of the malpais with the gold. Will was killed during the fight and one of Frank's lungs was pierced by an arrow. With the help of the guide, Frank made it to a government fort, possibly Wingate, and finally back home to Iowa.

Frank Lee told family members about their adventures in

New Mexico. Lee made it clear they had been in a box canyon where there was only one way in or out and that was through a narrow passage. They panned gold from the little stream; he was convinced it was the Lost Adams. He also said that the canyon was being guarded by renegade Indians and outlaws.

The gold they had taken from the canyon was buried near the spot where Will had died. It was near a small spring and Lee planned to return to collect it someday. But the wound in his lung led to poor health and finally he developed tuberculosis, dying in 1888. Before he died, he did provide maps and directions for the family.

The Lee family eventually left Iowa, moving to central Texas, but the stories told by Frank Lee were not forgotten. In the early 1890s Hudson's father made two trips into New Mexico. Although he was using the maps provided by Frank, both expeditions failed to find any gold. They couldn't locate the box canyon or the spring where Will had been buried.

Hudson also heard tales from William Donothan who claimed to have once been a sergeant in the Seventh Cavalry. Donothan researched the history of the Lost Adams and pointed out that Adams and his band of prospectors were not the first white men to find the canyon. Spaniards, according to the Apaches, had made several trips into the malpais, returning each time with gold. Finally the Apaches attacked them, killing them and burning the wagons where they stood. All that happened near the head waters of the San Francisco River where the U.S. Army later established Fort Tularosa.

Donothan claimed that during one of his scouting trips into the malpais, he found the remains of the Spanish massacre. Donothan said the remnants of the wagons were like those used by the conquistadors. Some even had arrowheads embedded in the rotting wood.

Donothan believed that in October 1926, he found the entrance to the Lost Adams. During one of his many trips, he came to a narrow canyon that had barbed wire strung across it. He thought it too plain a marker so he tore down the wire and buried it.

THE SECOND ADAMS PARTY

Donothan never had a chance to return to the narrow canyon, but he did learn more about the Lost Adams. He told Hudson that Adams and the party weren't freighters and prospectors as the legend stated but soldiers who had been discharged from the Army. The confusion was caused by a second man named Adams who, with a party of six men and women, were searching for the gold in 1885 or 1886. They, too, were led by a half-breed Apache who had some sort of a map.

Like the original Adams party, this one was ambushed by Indians and all were killed except for a man named Kelmere and one of the women. Both were wounded in the attack, but together they managed to get out. The woman's wounds were not as severe as Kelmere's so she helped him escape. They eventually made their way into Socorro.

Others who weren't searching for gold, but for lost cattle, stumbled onto the Lost Adams. Two cowboys working on the Jones ranch and chasing strays worked their way into a narrow canyon. The two separated and one of the men hadn't ridden very far when his horse bucked violently. He tried to force it forward, but the horse wouldn't approach a bush in their path. With his gun in hand, thinking there was a snake, he dismounted and saw a pair of boots sticking out from under the bush. The cowboy found the body of a man, shot through the head. Looking for identification, he found a thick, leather money belt stuffed with gold nuggets. The cowboy helped himself to a couple of the nuggets but decided that he wouldn't mention it to any of his fellow cowboys.

Back at camp his resolve collapsed. He showed them the nuggets. Although he told them all the details, he couldn't find his way back to the dead man. They tried to locate the body for months, but failed.

Clyde Brown, another El Paso cattle man, had a similar experience while working on the Nation's Ranch in the malpais country. As he chased a cow up a narrow canyon, he was confronted by an Indian. Brown quickly explained what he was doing and was ordered to get his cattle and get out. Farther up the canyon, he was again challenged and again told to get out.

After driving the strays from the canyon, Brown thought he would prevent a repeat. He strung barbwire across the entrance. That seems to be the source of the barbed wire that Donothan found and buried later that same year.

There are even more stories of the Lost Adams. Two or three people wandering in western New Mexico would periodically report finding the placer deposit. Some were looking for it when they found it and a few just stumbled onto it. Many claimed only to have seen the gold and some say they carried thousands of dollars out. One man living in Albuquerque supposedly had more than $30,000 on deposit in a local bank that came from the Lost Adams. The man remained unidentified to all except a few of the bank officers. His wealth, according to them, came from the malpais.

THE LOCATION OF THE LOST ADAMS

Adams always claimed that a prospector would never find the gold because it was hidden in the lava beds. According to Adams, in the distance, away from the cabin they had built, was a thick, rich vein of gold. The richest vein was at the foot of two rounded mountains. Donothan, Tolbert, and others believed that those mountains were the Sierra Brilante and Sierra Alto. Donothan claimed that the remains of the Spanish wagon train were at the foot of the Sierra Brilante. The cowboys who found the gold and a narrow canyon, and the archaeologist who saw the gold, were all in the old flow bed of the malpais west of Albuquerque. The ranch names, the descriptions, the mountain names, and the stories told by Adams all limit the area to be searched. All are sure of one thing. The gold is somewhere at the foot of two rounded mountains in the malpais.

There are those who believe they have found the mine today. The gold is gone, the waterfall is a trickle of water, and the cabin could never have been built because of the narrow passage. There is a short zigzag canyon, and a very narrow arroyo. But it doesn't fit the other clues left by Adams. There are no rounded mountains in the distance, and no lava beds close by. Those men believe it to be the site, they believe they have solved the mystery, but they are wrong. They located the Lost Adams in southern Arizona, but Adams was clear on several points. It was in the malpais, and it was in New Mexico—northwestern New Mexico, west and south of Albuquerque.

Today men and women still look for the gold first reported by Adams. The methods of search have changed. Armed with jeeps, airplanes, helicopters, geological maps, and metal detectors, they continue to comb the malpais of western New Mexico. Someday, one of those hunters might find the gold. Someday, one of them will find the canyon.

Or maybe the Apaches succeeded in hiding it as some said. Maybe those searching today walk over the top of the gold and never see it.

Or maybe Baxter and the others, who believe they found the Lost Adams, really did. Could it be that those monsoon storms that rake New Mexico in July and August flooded the canyon, washed tons of dirt down the arroyo, and buried the Lost Adams forever? The New Mexican landscape changes with the seasons and erodes with the rains. What is obvious one day, is gone the next, hidden under tons of dirt and debris.

So maybe the Lost Adams has been found. Maybe nature hid it better than the Apaches could ever hope. Or maybe, just maybe, the gold is right where so many thought it should be. And maybe, someday, some lucky person will find it, realize what it is, and become as wealthy as those who searched for it in the past believed they would become.

2

THE LOST
DUTCHMAN

—

ARIZONA

THE LOST DUTCHMAN IS ONE OF the few lost mines that is so close to civilization that a treasure hunter can spend the night in an air-conditioned hotel room and the day in the field. Room service, cable TV, and a comfortable bed make the search easier than it was just a few years ago. From the hotels of Mesa, Arizona, the Superstition Mountains can be seen when the haze has burned off the valley.

A short car ride down a six-lane highway and a two-lane road leads by Goldfield, housing a number of museums and tours, past the Lost Dutchman State Park, and to a turn off of the highway. By climbing to the top of the desert hill, the starting point for a search for the lost mine, Weaver's Needle, can be seen.

A hundred years ago that area of Arizona was rough. Men and women disappeared in the Superstitions regularly. Bodies of some were found, more often than not, dead by violence. Others were never seen again. Relatives waited for answers that never came.

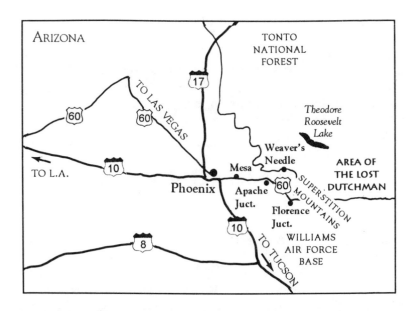

THE DUTCHMAN ARRIVES

The Dutchman arrived in Arizona in 1862, according to the census records. He lived in Arizona for about thirty years and died, according to the newspapers, on October 25, 1891, at the home of Mrs. Julia Thomas.

Mrs. Thomas, a woman who had been divorced and who operated an ice cream parlor in Phoenix, took care of the Dutchman in the last months of his life. Before he died, he told her about the fabulous mine he had found in the Superstition Mountains. It might have been in repayment for her kindness to him during his illness. After all, he would no longer be able to use the money.

The Dutchman, identified as Jacob Waltz (or Walls, or Walts or half a dozen other spellings), was actually a German. Those interested in that sort of thing have been able to trace him to Prussia, born around 1810. Nineteen or twenty years later, sometime around 1839, he emigrated to the United States, moving to the area around St. Louis, Missouri.

Ten years later, he moved on to California, apparently tempted by the stories of gold there. In an 1850 census taken in Sacramento, California, there is a J.W. Walls, who might be Jacob Waltz. In an 1860 census in Los Angeles County, Jacob Waltz appears, claiming to be a miner.

Other records from that period tell more about Waltz. On July 19, 1861, he was naturalized as a citizen of the United States. A year later, he had moved to Arizona, and in an 1864 census, he is listed as a miner who had lived in Yavapai County for two years. He then appears in Arizona records with regularity.

In September 1863, Waltz staked his first claim in Arizona in the area around Prescott. In March of the following year Waltz, and a number of others, signed a petition to Governor John N. Goodwin asking for protection from the Indians. This was in response to a March 2nd attack in which eight men were killed. Some of the miners, fearing further attacks, fled the area.

In September 1864, Waltz filed a few other claims in the Prescott area. There is no evidence that any of these claims ever produced any substantial amounts of gold. The mere fact that he registered claims in this area led some to speculate that the Lost Dutchman wasn't in the Superstitions as legend had it, but in the mountains near Prescott.

Some of the rumors claim that Waltz found the mine sometime in the 1870s. Rumors have been kept alive that Waltz enjoyed the high life in Phoenix, spending large amounts of money. Such rumors have underscored the value of the mine, but seem to have no basis. In fact, Waltz, according to the available records, lived a life that suggested he was very poor and almost always broke.

On August 8, 1878, after he had found the mine according to the legend and had gained untold wealth, Jacob Waltz was so poor that he sold everything he owned for fifty dollars to Andrew Starar. This agreement did one other thing. It effectively made Waltz, sixty-eight years old, the ward of another man. The question that must be asked is: If Waltz had access to the fabulous wealthy mine, why didn't he tap into that wealth instead of signing everything away?

WALTZ MENTIONED IN THE NEWSPAPER

In June 1884 Jacob Waltz is mentioned in the *Arizona Gazette*.

. . . yesterday word was received that a Mexican by the name of Pedro Ortega had been murdered, at the house of Jacob Waltz, a mile southeast of this city, by a man named Selso Grajalva. The matter was turned over to Justice Richards, who, acting as a coroner, summoned a jury and repaired to the scene of the tragedy at 1 o'clock. The Gazette reporter was on hand. He found the body of Ortega lying about thirty feet from the house of Jacob Waltz; his legs and abdomen from the knees to the breast bone were perforated with "double B" shot, the femoral artery on the right side being severed and in itself producing death. There is a mystery about the whole affair. Ortega was shot and killed by a shotgun belonging to Jacob Waltz. That gentleman heard the Mexicans talking loudly, and then the report of a gun. He ran to the side of the house where the tragedy occurred and saw the dying man.

The assassin evidently ran around the building in an opposite direction, returned the gun to the room and place from whence it had been taken, and then sought flight. Waltz did not know, and so testified at the inquest, that his gun had been the instrument of the crime until Deputy Sheriff Rogers appeared on the scene. . . . The murderer is still at large. . . .

Just months before his death, Waltz is again mentioned in the newspaper, this time concerning a flood in Phoenix. His house, not protected by an embankment, was swept away in the flood. That could explain why, when he died in October 1891, he was living in the house of Julia Thomas.

Waltz's life seems to be unremarkable. He traveled through the nineteenth century as so many others did, moving from Europe to New York and, finally, west. He searched for gold, filed claims, was involved in some violence, and then passed from the scene leaving nothing other than the story of wealth in the Superstition Mountains. He told Thomas where it was, and by doing so, moved from the ranks of the unknown to the famous.

THE LOCATION OF THE GOLD

The gold itself is believed to be in the Superstition Mountains, and, according to Thomas, somewhere near the landmark known as Weaver's Needle. Less than a year after the death of the Dutchman, Thomas was in the Superstitions with a small party, searching for the gold.

In a newspaper article published in the *Phoenix Gazette*, it was reported that "The story of the mine is founded upon the usual death bed revelations of the ancient miner usual in such cases."

That article is interesting because it contains some of the first published clues as to the actual location of the mine. "There is also a lost cabin connected with it. Its location is supposed to be a short distance back from the western end of the main Superstition mountains."

The question that lingers is where did all the gold come from? Is it, in fact, from a mine, or is it the remains of some kind of expedition? The region, after all, is one that was explored first by the Spanish, then by the Mexicans, and finally by the Americans. Indians had lived in the area for centuries and they knew what was of interest to the white men who came exploring.

Like so many other legends in the Southwest, the Lost Dutchman has its tale of massacre. A wealthy family in Mexico, the Peraltas, organized an expedition into Arizona in the 1840s before the Treaty of Hidalgo made the land part of the United States. Once that happened, access to the Superstition Mountains would be curtailed. It meant that the gold, once on Mexican territory, would now be in a foreign country.

According to the legend, hundreds of men, horses, mules, wagons, and tons of supplies crossed what would soon become the border, and drove north. They worked through the months, digging out the ore, separating it so that it could be better refined later. Rather than hauling out tons of worthless dirt, they worked it until it was mainly gold surrounded by some of the impurities. It was now extremely high-grade ore, something that could be transported for a huge profit.

However, they never got out of the Superstitions. The party was attacked, supposedly by Apaches, and wiped out. They hadn't been prepared for a good defense. They had been there to mine gold. Indian attacks had not been one of their major concerns.

But the Apaches did attack. Unaware of the importance of the yellow metal, and having no use for it, they ripped apart the sacks containing the gold, scattering it. They left it where it fell.

The story is that all members of the party were killed, but that presents a problem. If everyone was killed, then who told the story? First, there were family members who didn't accompany the expedition. Second, as always, there are rumors that one or two men did survive, eluding the Apaches and getting back to Mexico to tell of the fate of the expedition.

The sudden change in the Apache attitudes, and the violence of the attack, convinced the Peraltas to abandon the mine. There are stories that Don Miguel Peralta shared the secret of the Apache massacre with Jacob Waltz and that he gave Waltz enough information to find the scattered gold.

That means, of course, that the Lost Dutchman isn't a mine at all, but the remains of a mining operation by a large group of Mexicans. Waltz wasn't digging anything; he was picking up the gold the Apaches had dumped. The story of a mine would be the perfect cover for him. Anyone looking for a mine wouldn't expect to find the treasure already dug out, somewhat refined, and scattered on the open ground.

Waltz, with another German, Jacob Weiser, followed the map provided by Peralta. They approached the southern side of the Superstition Mountains and followed a long draw that led them to the interior. They found the Mexican's trail and worked their way past Weaver's Needle and finally into a deep, brush-choked canyon. The trail switched back and forth, finally ending at the mine.

As they arrived, they heard someone working in the distance. They approached carefully and spotted what they believed to be Apaches. Waltz and Weiser opened fire, killing three men. Hurrying forward, they discovered that they had killed three Mexicans. Frightened by what they had done, Waltz and Weiser gathered up the gold but then hurried away from the site. They just wanted to get away from there.

The shooting, however, attracted the attention of the Apaches. Before Waltz and Weiser could get clear, they were attacked by the Indians. In one version Weiser was killed. In another, he was seriously wounded and left by Waltz but eventually recovered, escaped from the Apaches, and worked his way to a friendly Indian village where he later died.

There were also those who believed that Waltz had killed Weiser, wanting all the gold for himself. There is additional evidence. Weiser, after reaching the Pima village, told his story to John D. Walker, who was living in a Pima village about eighteen miles from Florence, Arizona. Since Weiser apparently lived long enough to tell his story to Walker, there is some independent corroboration for the story of the lost mine. Most importantly, Weiser did not say that he had been shot by Waltz.

In 1881, Walker told his story to a newspaper editor, but there is no indication that anything about it was printed until after Waltz had died. According to various sources, the story told by Weiser was corroborated by Waltz. The description of the mine, and the location of it, are the same.

There is one other twist. In another version of the story, Weiser died in the fight with the Apaches in the Superstitions. He was buried there, near the mine. Find his grave, according to the legend, and the mine is close.

There are other stories, however, that suggest the existence of the mine or the treasure before Waltz entered the picture. One of the Arizona newspapers, dated February 15, 1878, claims that "Two Germans arrived in Florence on the 6th, from a prospecting tour through Superstition Mountain, where they found an extensive silver ledge, the ore from which assays over three thousand dollars to the ton. . . .The Germans who made the discovery, found, at the base of the mountain, on their way in, the remains of a white man, who evidently had been killed by Indians. . . . Many are preparing to visit the new silver fields."

Of course, this mentions a valuable find of silver and not gold. There are two Germans mentioned though neither are named. And the timing seems to be wrong for Jacob Waltz to be included in this. Finally, the find is reported months before Waltz signed away all his property. Had he been one of the Germans, it seems reasonable to believe that, rather than declare his personal bankruptcy, he would have used some of the silver discovered in the Superstitions.

What all this suggests is that Waltz found the mine or the gold sometime after 1878. There are stories that he had found the mine as early as 1848 or in 1862, which explains his move to Arizona. Fear of the Apaches might have kept him away from it when he needed money so badly in 1878.

The point is that Waltz knew something. Others seemed to have corroborated his story. Some talked of lost gold or mines in the Superstitions. In fact, there are a number of stories of different miners finding wealth and then losing it. One example is the Doctor Thorne Mine.

OTHER LOST MINES IN THE AREA

Doctor Abraham Thorne was an Army surgeon during the late nineteenth century stationed at Fort McDowell, near the Superstition Mountains. After curing several Apaches of some kind of an eye disease, they wanted to reward him. They blindfolded him and took him deep into the mountains. When they arrived at a specific spot, the Indians removed the doctor's blindfold and told him to gather as much of the gold as he could put into a small, leather pouch.

Thorne said it was apparent that the gold had already been partially refined. Thorne believed that the gold was not part of a natural deposit. As he was led from the area, he managed to catch a few glimpses of the surrounding territory. One of the few landmarks he did see was Weaver's Needle. He believed that the gold was no more than five miles from the base of the Needle.

Naturally, Thorne tried to find the gold himself. Circumstances prevented his quick return to the Superstitions. When he did get there, he couldn't find the right site. He searched for it, but was missing an essential piece of information, a specific landmark.

A few years after Waltz died, two more men stumbled onto gold in the Superstition Mountains. Miners named Silverlock and Malm shipped about fifteen thousand dollars worth of gold out of the mountains before their small vein played out. They apparently believed it was part of a rich outcropping and searched for the source of the gold but never found it. Again, many thought this was part of the Peralta gold.

Ten years after the Dutchman died, his mine was found again. Charlie Woolf said that he had stumbled on the mine about sixty miles from Florence. According to the story, he found a shaft, scattered miner's tools, and the skeletons of several dead men.

No reason is given for Woolf's failure to return to the mine, or why he didn't become a very rich man. The location of his mine, as reported in the newspaper, is wrong for the Lost Dutchman. He puts it a long way from Weaver's Needle and on the wrong side of the Salt River.

CON MEN ENTER
THE SEARCH

Twenty years later, the Lost Dutchman was found again. On August 20, 1920, the *Arizona Gazette* reported, "Word that ore assaying $408.40 to the ton has been uncovered in the famous 'Lost Dutchman' mine, situated within 60 miles of Phoenix and 4 miles southeast of Fish Creek hill, reached this city Friday, arousing much interest in mining circles.

"This report was verified by Dr. R.A. Aiton, secretary and treasurer of the company which is engaged in developing the 'Lost Dutchman' property, who spoke with the greatest enthusiasm of the latest news from the mine."

The story continued, reporting, "'This is the greatest gold strike in recent years in Arizona,' said Dr. Aiton. 'The Lost Dutchman mine, which was lost in reality for more than forty years, recently was rediscovered and now is in an active state of development. There is an immense ledge uncovered, and enough high grade ore to keep the mine in operation for countless years.

"'Operations will be pushed swiftly . . . and in the near future the company will build its own mill at a convenience site. . . .'"

This was a story that caught the imagination of all around it. The mine was found, the ore was good, but there was a suggestion that ore of an even higher grade would be recovered. There were necessary expenses such as improvements to the transportation system.

That is where the public came in. The Lost Dutchman Mining Corporation was formed with offices in Phoenix. There was a public stock offering to build sufficient capital so that the mine could be exploited. Those who wished to share in the wealth, but who had neither the time nor the ability to search for gold in the Superstition Mountains could now have a small share by investing risk capital. It wasn't much of a risk according to the newspaper because the mine had been found, the ore had been tested, and all that had to be done was for it to be taken from the ground.

Apparently there were a large number of investors who lined up. No one seemed to ask why—if they knew where the mine was, if the gold was there—they needed anyone else. Sure, development might take a little longer, but if the mine was as rich as they claimed, they didn't need outside investors.

They had some success in convincing investors that great wealth was just around the corner. However, the development of the mine never happened and the officers of the Lost Dutchman Mining Corporation skipped town with the money. It was clearly a scam.

In 1949 the Lost Dutchman was found again. According to the *Denver Post* of July 31, Henry H. Bruderlin of Los Angeles, using a map and a guide, discovered the gold. The *Post* reported:

> The century-old riddle of the location of the famed Lost Dutchman Mine in Arizona's Superstition Mountains was believed solved Saturday.
>
> Answer to the whereabouts of the lost mine for which scores of persons met violent death over the years was indicated in mining claims filed by Henry H. Bruderlin, 35, of West Los Angeles.
>
> Bruderlin's claims are to an area thrity-five miles east of Phoenix in the hills surrounding the myth-ridden Superstition Mountains. He thinks he has the original bonanza, last worked by the mad Dutchman, Jacob Walz [*sic*], in the middle of the last century.
>
> Bruderlin's luck began when he was given a map kept for years in the family records of [an] old Mexican family of Ray,

Arizona. Next he enlisted the aid of Jess Mullins, [a] 75-year-old prospector who has spent the last sixty years combing the Superstitions for gold.

Following the faded lines on the map, Bruderlin and Mullins were led about four miles out of the Superstitions proper and into the foothills where they picked up an ancient Spanish trail.

After that, Bruderlin said, it was merely a matter of following Spanish mining symbols hacked into saguaro cacti and chiseled onto scattered boulders.

The trail led to a hill set apart. Seven shafts were there—seven abandoned caved-in Spanish mining pits, Bruderlin told International News Service.

"It all seemed so simple—lifting the veil of a century. But it wasn't without thrills. We came to the top of a hill, and there they were—seven wonderful tumbled-in shafts. I forgot for the moment that this was the twentieth century."

Bruderlin was right. He had found the remains of Spanish mining operations in the area. He was wrong about it being the Lost Dutchman. In the end, he had discovered seven holes in the ground that contained no trace of gold or any other mineral of value. Eventually, his tale faded from public view.

In April 1975 the mine was found again. A man identified as Crazy Jake Jacob held a press conference to announce that he had found the fabulous Lost Dutchman Mine. According to Jacob, the mine was within sight of Weaver's Needle and had been covered with a mere eighteen inches of dirt. Jacob told Associated Press reporters that he had known exactly where he was going. He wasn't sure, at first, that he had found the Lost Dutchman. The final evidence, which convinced Jacob it was the Lost Dutchman, was found just prior to the press conference. The AP reporter noted that no gold had been displayed during the meeting with the press.

In January 1980 Charles Kentworthy reported that he had found the Lost Dutchman . . . again. According to him, using a variety of equipment, aerial photographs, and the Peralta Stone Maps, he located a number of "glory holes," that is, small deposits of gold and silver. Kentworthy didn't claim that he had located the Lost Dutchman, only that it was a real possibility that he had. He did say, tongue in cheek, that no one had put a sign on it.

A few weeks later, the Lost Dutchman was found, again. A lone man, ignoring the maps, legends, and rumors, found the mine by dowsing.

And, in February 1980, the Lost Dutchman was found once again. Charles Crawford told a reporter for the *Phoenix Gazette* that there was no doubt about it. He had found the mine in La Barge Canyon, exactly where the old maps said it would be. According to him, the mine was hidden under tons of rock from the cliffs above. Crawford claimed that the tailings dump assayed out at three ounces of gold per ton and that wasn't even in the mine.

Crawford apparently wasn't that interested in digging for treasure. Instead, he began to lecture at so much per person, telling his audience about his luck. He also organized tours into the area, allowing people to pan for gold on the site of the Lost Dutchman.

All of this is interesting and relatively harmless. A few people invested some money with Lost Dutchman Mining Corporation and lost it. Others held press conferences, had their fifteen minutes of fame, and vanished from the landscape. Some began to lecture about their discoveries, and led the unsuspecting into the mountains, where they could pan or dig for gold.

THOSE WHO HAVE DIED
IN THE SEARCH

But the legend of the Lost Dutchman also tells us that many people have been killed in the search. First, according to some of the legends, were the Mexicans who worked the area when it was still part of Mexico. Dozens were killed when the Apaches attacked them sometime in 1848.

Second, according to part of the legend, Waltz's partner, Weiser, died, either at the hands of the Indians, or Waltz himself.

And then those who followed behind began to lose their lives. No one knows how many loners traveled into the Superstition Mountains, died, and were never missed. The Arizona newspapers are full of stories of people disappearing or bodies being found. If nothing else is established as fact about the Lost Dutchman, this one thing is known. Many people have died trying to find it.

In June 1931, for example, Adolph Ruth arrived in Arizona with a map to the gold supposedly given to him by his son who got it from a relative of the Peraltas. The last time he was seen alive was when two cowboys left him in West Boulder Canyon. Half a year later an archaeological party found a human skull. It was believed that it was Ruth's.

In December 1931, the *Arizona Republic* reported:

[Deputy Sheriff Jeff] Adams will be in the mountains four or five days unless adverse weather conditions force him temporarily to abandon the search.... Adams and [W.A.] Barkley, will scour the vicinity in which the archaeological party found the skull in an attempt to locate the skeleton....

Ruth, 65 years old, disappeared in his search for the fabulously rich Lost Dutchman mine....

In 1947, James A. Cravey, 62 years old, was flown into the Superstition Mountains by helicopter. He had plenty of supplies but he vanished. Six months later, on February 21, 1948, his body was identified.

The *Arizona Republic* reported:

Discovery of James A. Cravey, sixty-two-year-old retired photographer, 114 West Polk Street, Phoenix, who disappeared in the rugged Superstition Mountains last June, while seeking the legendary Lost Dutchman Mine, was reported tonight by two Arizona visitors. They are Capt. R.F. Perrin, U.S. Army, retired, and Lt. Commander William F. Clements, of Chicago, guests of the Sunset Trail Ranch, eleven miles east of here (Phoenix). The two men reported finding the skeleton of a man minus the skull, late this afternoon, two and a half miles south of Weaver's Needle, while on an all- day hike in the area. Because of the hour, they did not search for the skull but brought the man's wallet back to Sunset Trail Ranch. . . .

Both the men, according to the investigations carried out at the time, had been shot and then decapitated. The skulls had been removed by a human agency. This conclusion was based on the fact that both skulls were so far from the remainder of the skeletons. Animals might have scattered the bones but they wouldn't have moved them long distances.

Bernardo Flores was 55 years old when he disappeared after he had gone in search of the Lost Dutchman. His skeleton was found but his skull was missing.

On October 23, 1960, an Australian exchange student's skeleton was found. The remains were later identified as those of Franz Harrier. The skull was about seventy feet from the body. He'd been shot through the head twice.

In June 1961 Jay Clapp disappeared. He had been living in a cave for eleven years and was last seen when a deputy sheriff gave him a ride. His mother had sent him a check every two weeks and when she arrived to look for her son, five of the checks were unclaimed.

Clapp's skeleton was found three years later. No cause of death could be determined from the remains. All that was observed was that the skull was not with the rest of the remains.

The skeletons of others were found with the skulls near the other bones. On February 24, 1955, the skeleton of Charles Massey was found. Massey had been shot between the eyes.

In April 1955 four boys entered the Superstitions to hunt wild pigs. One of the boys was separated from the group and when he didn't show up at camp later that evening, the other boys called the sheriff. The following day, the boy's body was found at the base of a cliff. He had been shot through the head.

About a year later, Martin G. Zywotho of Brooklyn, New York was found with a bullet hole in his head. The coroner's jury ruled the death accidental, or a possible suicide.

There are, of course, a long list of names of those who just vanished. The terrain is rough, with few roads. Those who walk in without training, proper equipment, and a map that will lead them to riches are ill prepared for what they find. Add to that someone who seems to be guarding something valuable, who wants no one around, and it isn't surprising that so many have vanished.

But the murders go back to the turn of the century. If this wasn't the modern United States, if this wasn't within sight of Mesa and Phoenix, explanations might be simple. But for over ninety years men and women have been killed in the Superstitions. Others have vanished. Court records show that none of these crimes have been solved and no one has been prosecuted for them.

There are some exceptions occurring when partners have had a falling out. In 1959 Stanley Fernandez was shot and killed by Benjamin Ferreira, apparently while he was asleep in his sleeping bag. He pled guilty to manslaughter and was sentenced to the Arizona State Prison. Released on parole, he returned to his home in Hawaii and eventually killed his mother-in-law.

Others have been gunned down, and in one case the "Code of the West" seems to have been applied. When Ed Piper shot and killed Robert St. Marie in 1959, he was not prosecuted. The Arizona authorities decided that Piper had acted legally in self-defense.

THE PAPER TRAIL

There is a long list of those killed, many shot, associated with the Lost Dutchman. That has led some to speculate that someone found the mine and killed those who got too close. The problem with that theory is that it would have to be a discovery handed down from generation to generation because the murders go back nearly a century. Second, there is no record that large amounts of gold have been mined and then shipped from the area. Such records would create a paper trail back to the Superstitions. No paper trail has been found.

One researcher, attempting to document the existence of great wealth claimed that he had found records at the Sacramento Mint proving that Waltz had shipped just over a quarter of a million dollars in gold to the mint. It was all documented for anyone to see.

Of course there never was a mint in Sacramento. At the time that Waltz allegedly shipped all that gold, mints existed in Carson City, Nevada; San Francisco, California; Denver, Colorado;

New Orleans, Lousiana; and Philadelphia, Pennsylvania. Records of searches there and at various archives have failed to produce any evidence that Waltz had shipped any gold to the mints.

This means, simply, that no documentation exists for gold being shipped to the mints. It doesn't mean the mine didn't exist or that the gold didn't exist. Someone, or a number of someones, in the Superstition Mountains is protecting something. It might be that they believe they have the right track, but have yet to discover the mine. They want no one else to search for it, so they can find it first.

But the main question has yet to be answered: Was there ever a Lost Dutchman Mine? The answer to that specific question is probably no. There never was a Lost Dutchman Mine, and if there was, it is gone now.

THE EARTHQUAKE

At 2:35 P.M., local time, an earthquake hit the area. The *Arizona Weekly Enterprise* reported, ". . . we had quite a sharp shock of earthquake here. . . . Large pieces of rock were detached on all sides of Picket Post mountain, which of course rolled to the bottom, raising a cloud of dust. . . ."

If the Dutchman had found his mine prior to the earthquake on May 3, 1887, then it might have disappeared. Landmarks were radically changed, mine shafts collapsed, and the arroyos and valley were sudden filled with tons of rock and dirt. The rich mine would be gone.

There is one other consideration. Maybe Waltz never had the mine but had found the Peralta "massacre gold." He may have known where it had been scattered by the Apaches and would visit the area, picking up a little of it to use in his daily life. In those days gold nuggets and small bags of gold dust were often traded for groceries and other necessities. If Waltz had a large amount of gold, he would have had to deal with someone who could handle it. No evidence exists to show that he did.

Again, according to the best evidence, the massacre gold was scattered in 1848 when the Peralta party was attacked. That gold, which had lain in the open for nearly forty years, might have been covered by the earthquake in 1887. Waltz would have known where it was and where to dig to find it, if it had been buried in the earthquake. Now, instead of easy access to the gold, he would have had to work to get it.

So, when he shared the information with Julia Thomas, he told her he had a secret mine. It wasn't a mine in the classic sense, but the result of someone else's work. The point is, there was gold.

THE PERALTA STONES

That then brings up the next question: Is there any basis for the story of the Peralta mining in Arizona? Is the story of the Apache massacre true?

A series of stone maps were found by a man from Oregon about thirty years ago. He, along with his family, had pulled off a road on the southern approach to the Superstition Mountains. Not far from the car he discovered three carved stones. These have been interpreted as being a map, or directions, that would lead to the Peralta gold.

Analysis, however, suggests the stones were carved just before they were found. And the location, so close to a road, makes it unlikely they had been there for very long. It seems to be a hoax, perpetrated by someone who wanted to stir up interest in the Lost Dutchman.

Charles W. Polzer, a Jesuit ethnohistorian, analyzed the stones, and declared that he had some serious reservations about their authenticity. First, he noticed that the stone surface was not rough. The carving on the stones seemed to have been made by sharp, twentieth-century tools, and not those of a hundred years earlier.

Analysis of the contents of the carvings also suggest a twentieth-century hand. The "type" style, that is, the letters themselves, are more consistent with those used in today's American world than in the Mexican world of the last century.

All things considered, it seems that the Peralta stones are just another in a long line of hoaxes perpetrated on those who want to believe in the Lost Dutchman Mine.

THE FINAL ANSWER

Given what we know, given all the information that has been published since the death of Jacob Waltz, it seems reasonable to believe there was gold. It might not be the fabulously wealthy mine of the legend, but it did exist, in some form. Other mining operations in the area, and a rich history from the Spanish past, all contribute to that belief.

But remember one thing. There was the earthquake in 1887. If Waltz found gold from the Peralta massacre, it is now buried. If he had a mine, it probably collapsed. However, the gold wasn't destroyed. It may still be out there.

3

THE LOST PEGLEG

—

CALIFORNIA AND NEVADA

THIS STORY IS PROBLEMATIC DUE to the fact that there are so many additional complications. There is talk that Pegleg Smith found two seperate gold deposits and lost both of them. There is talk that one man couldn't have done everything that Smith is alleged to have done, so there must have been two men. And there is talk that the lost placer mines are not in California or Nevada but actually in Arizona or Colorado. Nothing like narrowing the search with precise information.

The best evidence, however, suggests that the Lost Pegleg is at the confluence of the Virgin River and the Colorado River under what is now Lake Mead. The search area can be found only with the use of scuba gear.

The story begins in 1827 when Pegleg Smith, along with a number of other hunters, entered the southwest to trap beaver. They reached an area near where Needles, California is today, fought with the Indians there, and then escaped. The Indians chased them until the trappers turned around, killing many of the Indians who had followed them.

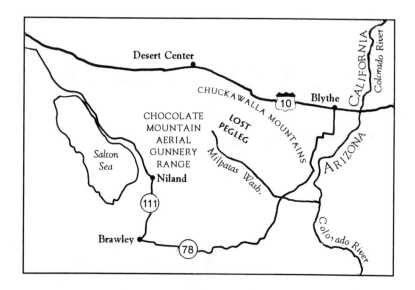

With the problem solved, they returned to their search for beaver and established a camp along the Virgin River. Another trapper soon arrived with several pouches filled with gold nuggets. Pegleg Smith identified the metal as copper. Pegleg then used the metal to cast bullets for the whole trapping party.

Smith thought nothing more about it until two decades later. Now he was in the gold fields of California and had a chance to examine the nuggets of the placer gold deposits. He realized that it hadn't been copper that he had used to make the bullets so long ago. It had been gold. Thick, heavy nuggets from a very rich placer deposit. Best of all, Pegleg knew the approximate location of the gold.

Smith gathered a party of men, telling them of the gold, and they headed out. Disputes broke out quickly and by the time they reached the search area, only nine men remained with the party. They searched for a month but failed to find anything of value.

When John C. Fremont passed through the area, the men joined his party and returned to California.

Pegleg searched again for the gold, but never found it. Smith died in 1866 without a penny to his name. Most thought he was a liar of the first magnitude.

Many small placer deposits dotted the West. The vulgarities of the rivers and weather uncovered them for a short period and then hid them again. This story is interesting because the men misidentified the gold as copper and then used the metal to make bullets.

For those who wish to search, the best area is around the Virgin River and Colorado River near Lake Mead. Although the original deposit might be under water, there is a good chance that the gold had been moved down to the area from farther up the Virgin River. That might be the best place to search for it. Or, it is just possible that the gold might be lost forever.

4

THE LOST
SUBLETT

—

TEXAS

SOME GEOLOGISTS SAY THAT there are no naturally occurring gold deposits in the Guadalupe Mountains. Others suggest that new findings, new surveys, suggest that gold might be found there. And there is always the possibility that someone carried the gold in and hid it in a cave for some unknown reason.

William Caldwell Sublett, know as Ben, claimed that he had found gold in the Guadalupe Mountains. Having lived poor most of his life, toward the end he seemed to have access to large amounts of gold, which he used to pay his bills and surprise his friends.

Sublett grew up in Tennessee. He wandered from job to job, first in Missouri and then on to Colorado and finally into west Texas. He married Laura Louise Denny and eventually had three children, two girls and one son.

They settled in Monahans, Texas where Ben took odd jobs when he could, and Laura did laundry. They lived on the outskirts

Note:
Sublett travelled
from Odessa into
the Guadalupes to
find his gold.

of town, in the back of a wagon and a tent. Life was hard and the jobs few. Finally they moved to Odessa where life took on the same pattern.

But Laura was sick with tuberculosis. Shortly after the birth of the third child, the boy Rolth, she died. The oldest daughter took over the duties of mother and laundress. Ben followed his old pattern of taking odd jobs when he could find them, and prospecting in the Guadalupe Mountains when he felt he could.

On one of the jobs he found himself working with an old Apache Indian. During a break in the work, Sublett told of his prospecting. The Apache said that he knew of a rich mine hidden in the Guadalupes. Sublett pressed for details. With the help of the Indian, he was able to draw a rough map so that he could find the gold.

Now his trips into the mountains became more frequent. He was ignoring his children, allowing the oldest daughter responsibility for raising her sister and brother. The only income came from her work as a laundress and family finances were quickly eroded.

While Ben was in the mountains, the community decided that someone had to help the children. They were removed from the rough shack and placed in foster homes. Within days Ben was back in Odessa but this time he had gold. His first stop was a local saloon where he bought the house a round.

With his newfound wealth, he gathered his children, provided a better home for them, and bought them new clothes and toys. But it wasn't long before he was as broke as he had always been. This time, however, there was a difference.

Ben hitched his wagon and disappeared for a couple of days. When he returned he had more gold. It was described as so pure that a jeweler could use it without any additional refining. It was extremely high-grade ore.

It became obvious to the residents of Odessa that Sublett had found a very rich gold deposit. They would wait for his trips into the mountains so they could follow. Ben would leave late at night or early in the morning and travel in circles. He would camp for days on end. Somehow he always managed to lose even the most tenacious of trackers. And somehow he always managed to return to Odessa with a couple of small pouches filled with rich gold nuggets.

Sublett had a bank account in nearby Midland, Texas. W.E. Connell, who owned the bank, said that whenever his funds ran low, Sublett would travel into the mountains and return to deposit cash in the bank. Connell didn't know where he exchanged the gold for cash.

Connell and a Midland rancher, George Gray, tried to convince Ben to tell them the location of the mine. They offered him ten thousand dollars for the information. Sublett laughed

and pointed out that he picked up more than that in a long afternoon of prospecting.

Connell and Gray convinced an experienced tracker to help
them, but Ben lost the man during his wanderings. He returned
to Odessa with gold and the tracker came in a few days later, tired
and angry.

Ben did reveal the location to a couple of people. One, a
local prospector known to most only as Grizzly Bill, was taken
into the Guadalupes. Grizzly Bill stopped at a tavern in Pecos
afterward and bought drinks for everyone. He bought himself
more than a few, and began bragging about his newfound wealth.
During the course of the celebration, Bill was talked into a
bronco riding contest, during which he was killed.

Mike Wilson was also given the location of the mine. Like
Grizzly Bill, he was so excited about his wealth that he bought drinks
for everyone at a local tavern. He ran through the money quickly
and in just a couple of days found himself broke. He traveled back to
the Guadalupes but confused the landmarks. He couldn't find the
mine and asked Ben to show him again where it was.

Sublett was outraged by Wilson's attitude. He told Wilson
that he didn't deserve to know the location. Ben would not invite
him on any more trips and Wilson spent the rest of his life trying
to find the gold.

Sublett also showed the location to his son, Rolth. The boy
was nine at the time and more interested in other things. He didn't
pay attention to the landmarks or the canyon where the gold was
hidden. When his father tried to lower him into the mine shaft to
show him the riches there, the boy was frightened by the dark.

Ben always said that there was more gold in the mine than he
could use in a lifetime. It was going to be his legacy to his family.
But that wasn't meant to be. When Rolth was fourteen, his father
became sick. Rolth was with his father during those last days and

asked for directions to the mine. He asked for the landmarks, but was told he would never find it unless he was shown again. Sublett died, apparently with no one knowing the exact location of his riches.

There is other corroboration for this tale from those who saw the gold and heard the stories. Rufus Stewart said that while working as a guide, he was camped with a party near the Pecos River. Sublett arrived at the camp and was invited to have coffee. Stewart knew Ben from Odessa and had heard the stories. Sublett invited Stewart to go with him, but Stewart said he had to remain with the men he'd promised to guide.

As Ben rode out the next morning, he tried to show Stewart the location. Through a telescope Stewart watched Ben disappear into the distance. Sublett found Stewart on his return and showed him a large quantity of gold.

In 1892 Sublett died with little in the bank. His illness ate at his resources and his burial took a large chunk of what was left. Rolth buried his father and used all the money that remained in an expedition to find the mine.

The problem was that he had only been nine when his father showed him the gold and he couldn't be bothered with landmarks and trails. He wanted to get where they were going.

Now his sisters were married and, though they might have been interested in the gold if they had known where it was, they had their own lives to live. Rolth was alone in Odessa, knowing that somewhere in the Guadalupe Mountains was a rich mine that could make him a wealthy man.

His first trip into the mountains was a failure. There were landmarks that looked familiar but he couldn't find the right canyon. When his food was gone, he returned to Odessa and fell into the pattern that would mark the rest of his life. He would take odd jobs to raise a stake and then head out into the mountains.

There were investors. Those living in Pine Springs, Texas, near the point where Rolth entered the mountains, saw him often. He would introduce the locals to his friends and then they would drive off in search of the gold.

Rolth turned the search into his life's work. There was always someone who was willing to pay for the hunting trips, someone who would provide money for Rolth's living expenses and pay him a wage while they hunted for his father's mine. A few people thought that he kept the legend alive for that reason alone.

Rolth never found his father's mine. He had been in it once and had lived off the gold as a kid. But when he had his one chance to learn the exact location, he had been interested in too many other things.

The Lost Sublett differs from other legends in a couple of ways. First, there is no tale of an Indian massacre of Spanish explorers. There are no tales of stacks of gold bars and bones of dead guards. Instead, it seems to consist of a rich deposit of gold nuggets that contain little impurity. And, most importantly, Ben Sublett never tried to find others to finance his expeditions into the mountains. He knew that the gold itself would finance anything he needed.

Finally, there are the interesting stories told by Odessa and Midland residents. In those two west Texas towns there seems to be a rich history of bank records and newspaper accounts that tend to corroborate points of Sublett's story.

If there is a single true tale of a lost mine, this is it. Even the latest geological surveys suggest there are some areas in the Guadalupe Mountains where gold can be found. And apparently, in one of those areas, Ben Sublett found it.

The gold and the mine are still there. Sublett probably concealed the entrance to the shaft so it would be difficult for others to find. More than a hundred years have passed but the gold is still there for some lucky person.

5

THE SILVER BULLETS

—

ARKANSAS

TOBE INMON, A POOR FARMER IN Kentucky, had a life filled with hard luck and constant change. After he had a run-in with a neighbor, who said that Inmon had stolen some livestock, Inmon had nothing to hold him in Kentucky. He loaded his family in his wagon and they headed west.

He finally arrived in Pope County, Arkansas, at the Moccasin Creek Valley. There he built a small cabin for his family and began his farming operation.

The nearest town was Dover, Arkansas. People there remembered him as an antisocial man who had little to say and never lingered to visit friends. His clothing was no more than rags and, when his family was in town, they dressed in the same fashion. It was clear that Inmon had no money and was barely scraping by on his farm.

Sometime during the fall of 1903, one of Inmon's children took sick. Neither he nor his wife could do a thing for the boy. Inmon

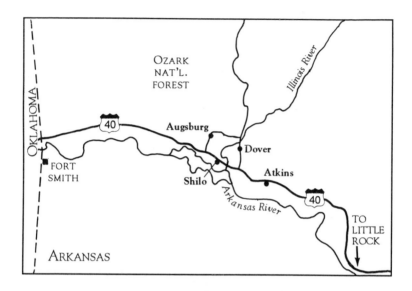

rushed into town and asked the doctor for help. Benjamin Martin, the only doctor in the area, followed Inmon back out to the cabin.

It took two days for the fever to break, but break it did. The boy began to recover and Inmon wanted to know what he owed Martin for his help. Martin said that Inmon could pay him later, when things were a little better for the family.

Inmon didn't want to owe any debt to any man. He held out a bag of bullets, saying that the doctor should take them as partial payment. Ammunition was important to nearly everyone in that area at the time, so Martin gladly accepted the bullets. Inmon said that he had made them himself, from iron that he had found in an old shaft at the back of his property.

The bullets looked to be well made and Martin planned to use them on his next hunting trip but, overwhelmed with work, Martin delayed the trip. The bag was pushed to the back of a shelf and forgotten for nearly two years.

Planning another hunting trip two years later, he took the bullets down and put them on his desk. He scraped at the black on the nose of one of the bullets and it rubbed off, revealing a shiny metal that didn't look like iron to Martin.

Instead of going hunting, Martin went to the larger village of Russellville. There, a friend examined the bullets and told him they were made from silver. Martin sold the sack to the man for seventy-two dollars.

Martin returned to his house with plans to visit Inmon in the morning. He'd have Inmon show him the shaft and tell him that it was silver, not iron. Inmon, who had been living so poor, in a one room cabin that was more of a shack than a house, had been sitting on a silver mine and obviously didn't know it.

The Inmons were gone when the doctor arrived. Neighbors didn't know where, though some suggested they had moved to Texas. Martin shrugged and walked out behind the cabin, climbed the hills, and searched for the shaft that Inmon had told him was there. He failed to find it.

A few days later, with a wagon of supplies, Martin moved into the cabin. He searched the area during the day, staying in the decaying shack at night. When his food ran out he returned to Dover, but only long enough to buy additional food and supplies.

Martin returned to the shack many times. He let his practice die and became obsessed with finding the silver shaft. Friends said that the search drove him insane.

After Martin died, as the rumors of the lost mine circulated throughout the area, treasure hunters actively began to search for it. Someone found a cache of very old Spanish mining tools, which led to rumors that the lost mine had originally been worked by the Spanish. Historical evidence did confirm that the Spanish had explored the region hundreds of years earlier. But there was no evidence that the Spanish had ever worked any mines there.

In 1951, an old Cherokee Indian named Lawrence Mankiller sold a large silver nugget in Fort Smith, Arkansas. Mankiller told those interested that he had found the nugget in the entrance to an old mine shaft in the Moccasin Creek area where he was hunting deer.

Mankiller was asked if he would show a group of men where he had found the silver nugget and he agreed. They paid him several hundred dollars to lead them to the shaft the next day. But when the sun came up Mankiller was gone, along with his fee.

There have been silver deposits found in that general area over the years. There is no question that silver mines and silver veins have been found. Some played out quickly but others produced hundreds of thousands of dollars.

And there is no doubt that the Spanish worked the area hundreds of years earlier. The great distance to the oceans, problems with transportation, and hostile natives all worked against the Spanish. Stories of Spanish treasures hidden throughout the United States exist and Arkansas is no exception.

There is one other aspect to this legend. Several people have reported seeing strange night lights over the hills in the Moccasin Creek Valley region. Some believe that the lights hover over deposits of gold and silver, guarding them from those not worthy to own the treasure.

None of that makes any real difference. The Tobe Inmon Lost Mine may still be there. Dr. Martin might have walked past it a dozen times. Someone might have already found it and taken the treasure from it. There is one thing that is clear, however. Tobe Inmon's luck was so bad that when he finally did strike it rich, he didn't know it.

PART II

HIDDEN
TREASURES

6

THE TREASURE OF OAK ISLAND

—

NOVA SCOTIA

THERE ARE A FEW CASES WHERE the exact location of the treasure is known. Most of the time, it is a shipwreck where the depth of the water or the shifting of the silt on a river bottom have created problems for those trying to recover the loot. In one case, on Oak Island, the exact location of the horde is known down to the millimeter. Everyone knows precisely where the treasure is, even how deep it is buried, but no one knows how to get to it.

The story begins in October 1795 when three teenagers rowed across Mahone Bay to land on the shore of tiny, wooded Oak Island. Anthony Vaughan, Dan McGinnis, and Jack (John) Smith decided to look around before eating their lunch. They found a clearing where a single oak towered over the open area. They noticed that a limb had been sawed off, that the stump showed evidence of ropes and tackle, and that directly below it was a circular depression about twelve or fifteen feet in diameter. To the teenagers it looked as if something had been buried there long before.

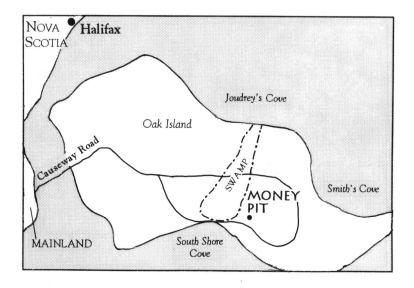

Or the story might have begun as early as June 1795. D'Arcy O'Connor reports in *The Big Dig: The $10 Million Search for Oak Island's Legendary Treasure* that John Smith purchased Lot 18 on June 26, 1795. Lot 18 is, of course, the location of what was to become known as the Money Pit.

The boys knew that pirates had once roamed the area. They thought of chests filled with gold, and pots of gems collected from around the region. There were stories of lost treasure in the area and the boys believed they might have found one of those hidden caches.

The next day, when they returned to the island, but this time they brought shovels and picks. As they began to dig, they realized that someone else had dug there sometime before. The shovels slipped into the earth easily. That would suggest that whatever was hidden, hadn't been there long, certainly no more than a decade or two.

Only two feet down, they ran into the first real proof of something extraordinary. They found a layer of flagstones, which later investigation showed had come from the Gold River, about two miles up the coast on the mainland.

Ten feet down they came to a layer of oak logs. They broke through it, but found nothing more than more dirt. They continued to dig. They discovered a boatswain's whistle and a copper coin dated 1713. Sure that they had found the site of a buried fortune, they continued to dig.

At twenty feet, they hit another layer of oak logs. They broke through it quickly so they could continue. They noticed that the pit was about thirteen feet in diameter and that the sides were made of hard clay that showed pick marks, while the dirt in the center was soft and easy to dig through. Below the wooden platform, the ground had settled, leaving a two-foot gap.

At thirty feet they found another layer of logs. Convinced the treasure had to be close, they broke through the platform and were again disappointed. They found only more dirt.

At this point they knew that the task would require expert help. They had dug down as far as they could without some kind of assistance. They failed to find help because the farmers and fishermen on the mainland already had enough work to keep them busy. Besides, many of those living on the mainland had seen strange night lights on the island for many years and they were afraid of what might be hidden there; or who might be watching.

Smith, who was married, moved onto the island, where he farmed for many years and watched the treasure pit. His fellow treasure hunter, McGinnis, also farmed on the island. Both hoped to one day solve the mystery and be wealthy by recovering the treasure.

SYNDICATES ENTER
THE SEARCH

Nothing happened after the initial interest in 1795 until Simeon Lynds heard the story of the pit and the wealth it promised. He was so excited by what he heard that he formed a company, financed by thirty fellow businessmen, to excavate the Money Pit. The syndicate was called the Onslow Group.

The syndicate's dig began again in 1803. Their first task was to dig out the debris that had fallen into the pit in the eight years since any work had been done. In short order they were down to the thirty-foot level reached by Vaughan, McGinnis, and Smith and, by the middle of the summer, had dug out another sixty feet.

Every ten feet they hit a layer of logs, but at sixty feet they began to find other debris as well. Some of the log layers were reinforced by charcoal and putty and a strange fibrous material that was later identified as coconut husks. The closest coconut tree is more than a thousand miles from Oak Island.

At ninety feet, on the log layer, the workers found a stone slab that contained a strange inscription. Some sixty years later, about 1865, a professor claimed to have finally decoded the message on the stone. It said, "Forty feet below, two million pounds are buried." The code wasn't particularly clever and it's not explained why it took so long to decipher.

Others are skeptical of the translation, saying that about the time the professor figured it out, a syndicate was formed to sell stock in a company to recover the treasure. Descriptions of the stone have been reported in all the early accounts of the Money Pit, and hundreds, if not thousands, were reported to have seen it, so there is no doubt that such a stone did exist. It was described as about two feet long, fifteen inches wide, and ten inches thick. It weighed about 175 pounds. It disappeared in 1919.

They pulled the slab out of the pit, broke through the wooden platform, and kept on digging. The pit had originally been dry, but now water was beginning to seep into it. The workers were taking out almost as much water as dirt, but no one was concerned about it at that time. They probed the bottom with a metal rod, and at ninety-eight feet, hit something that a few of them thought might be a chest. With darkness coming, however, they were forced to stop work for the night.

When they returned the next day they found the pit now filled with water. They began to bail it out, working steadily through the morning. After several hours they noticed they were making no real progress. The water level had not been lowered at all.

They abandoned their efforts for the year: It was late summer and the men had to return to their farms. The company officers planned to come back the following year and finish the quest for the treasure.

In 1804, they went back and confirmed that it was impossible to bail out the pit. They decided to dig another hole not far from the original pit, and then tunnel over to it, defeating the water by sneaking up on it.

They dug down more than 114 feet and then began to tunnel. Before they could break through to the Money Pit, water began to seep through the ground slowly and then it began to flood. The men were forced from the pit as the wall between the new pit and the old collapsed. Soon the water stood at the same level in both pits.

With that, they were forced to abandon their attempts. They realized that no amount of bailing would ever drain the water. The treasure, which they were sure was down there, was just beyond their reach.

Smith, who still lived on the island, went back to farming. At some point he filled in both the pits. Although there were local legends about the treasure, and it seems that almost everyone in Nova Scotia was aware of the stories, no one could think of a way to defeat the booby traps that protected the Money Pit.

THE SEARCH CONTINUES

In 1849 another corporation was formed to try to recover the treasure. Called the Truro Company, they thought that they could get down to the treasure. Dan McGinnis had died, but both Smith and Vaughan were still alive. One of them, probably Vaughan, showed the Truro Company engineers where the original Money Pit had been.

Once again they began to dig. In less than two weeks they were down about eighty feet. At that point, the water began to seep in again, and the workers were forced out. In an hour or two, the pit was again filled to the same level as before.

The company was forced to abandon the attempt, but returned a few days later to erect a platform about thirty feet down, just above the water level. From there, using an auger, they explored as best they could. They confirmed a layer of wood at ninety-eight feet that was five inches thick, just as the early Onslow Group had found. Below that was an open space and then came the interesting discoveries, reported in a letter sent by Jothan B. McCully:

> . . . the auger dropped 12 inches and then went through four inches of oak; then it went through five inches of metal in pieces, but the auger failed to take any of it in except three

links, resembling an ancient watch chain. It then went through eight inches of oak, which was thought to be the bottom of the first box and the top of the next; then 22 inches of metal, the same as before [meaning loose], then four inches of oak and six inches of spruce; then into clay seven feet without striking anything else. . . . On withdrawing the auger, several splinters of oak, such as might come from the side of an oak stave, and a small quantity of a brown fibrous substance, closely resembling the husk of a coconut, were brought up.

For the first time there was real evidence that something had been hidden at the bottom of the Money Pit, and that it was still down there. The gold chain links suggested a treasure, as did the loose metal, possibly coins. They were unable to recover anything else from the Money Pit, but the findings did excite them.

With these results, the Truro Company drilled several additional holes in the bottom of the pit but didn't find anything else as intriquing. Or rather, something was found, but the two men who knew what it was never reported publicly on it.

John Pitbladdo was the foreman on the crew. He inspected the bit and the core samples as they were brought back to the surface. John Gammell, a major shareholder in Truro, visited the site one afternoon and saw Pitbladdo slip something from the drill bit into his pocket. Gammell asked what it was but Pitbladdo said he would provide a full report at the next shareholders' meeting. He didn't want to provide one man with an advantage over his fellow stockholders.

A NEW COMPANY IS FORMED

Records show that on August 1, 1849, Pitbladdo and Charles D. Archibald applied to the lieutenant general of the province for a license to dig for treasure on Oak Island. They received the permission but it was limited to unoccupied and ungranted lands on the island. They then tried to buy all the land on Oak Island owned by John Smith. That is, they tried to buy the site of the Money Pit.

Pitbladdo never reported to the Truro shareholders what he had found that day. His sudden attempts to buy the land and dig for the treasure himself suggest that he was convinced of the great wealth hidden in the pit. Pitbladdo is rumored to have died shortly after this. It has also been suggested that he left the area and went on to other jobs as a mining engineer. There is a reference to a James Pitblado who was supervisor of mining in Chester in 1875 and some Oak Island accounts refer to a James Pitblado. Pitbladdo disappears from the Oak Island story shortly after his aborted attempt to buy the land and get to the treasure.

In 1850 the Truro Company decided to dig another shaft to the northwest of the original Money Pit. They hoped to tunnel to the treasure, as had others, or failing that, to use the new shaft as a way of pumping the water from the Money Pit. As before, they dug down just over a hundred feet and then began to work their way toward the treasure. They reached a point that was nearly under the Money Pit, or that they believed was under it, when water burst through, sending the workers fleeing again. In a matter of minutes the new shaft was filled with water just as all the others had been.

As planned, they began pumping operations, which succeeded in lowering the level of the water slightly. It was obvious that a huge volume of water was entering the pit by design. The two other shafts, dug through clay, had been dry until workers began attempts to tunnel into the Money Pit and the water now in those shafts was coming directly from the Money Pit itself. The water was not from a natural spring; it was some sort of booby trap that Vaughn, McGinnis, and Smith tripped in their attempt to reach the treasure early on.

THE BOOBY TRAPS ARE DISCOVERED

Someone finally noticed that the level of the water in the Money Pit seemed to rise and fall with the tide in the bay. Someone else noticed that a small stream of salt water emptied into Smith's Cove at low tide. Searching, they found that the beach there was not natural, but an artificial creation. Digging through the sand, they found a layer of coconut fiber and eel grass that was protecting an area of loose fitting stone.

The next plan was to build a cofferdam out away from the beach. When that was completed, they tore up the whole beach and discovered a network of drains that sloped slightly downward. One by one, they began to destroy the drains until an Atlantic gale swept away their cofferdam before they could complete that work.

They believed that all the drains emptied into a single shaft that let the water flow into the Money Pit. If they could find the shaft and block it, they would be able to stop the flow of water and get at the treasure.

About a hundred feet from the beach of Smith's Cove, on a line with the Money Pit, they began to dig; but when they reached a level of about seventy-five feet, decided they had miscalculated and missed the shaft. They moved twelve feet to the south and began another attempt. At thirty-five feet they hit a large boulder, which they began to pry out when the new shaft filled with water. They had found the path of the water.

To block this drain, they partially refilled their pit and drove wooden pilings through the bottom to create a makeshift dam. Satisfied that they had blocked the water flow, they returned to the pumps but still couldn't reduce the level of the water significantly. It meant they had either failed to completely block the drain from Smith's Cove, or there was another drain system hidden somewhere else they had failed to find.

They tried another shaft, digging down to 112 feet before it flooded. Now they were out of time; the summer had ended and the weather was beginning to turn cold. More importantly, they were out of money.

In 1851, the Truro Group tried to raise more money to begin another assault on the Money Pit, but the investors refused. They'd already spent enough money, and though they'd found evidence that there was a treasure at the bottom of the pit, they couldn't defeat the elaborate booby traps set by those who had buried it.

They had learned a great deal. The coconut husks and eel grass spread over the drainage system were designed to prevent silting. Coconut resisted the effects of the salt water, and had been used for hundreds of years in ships as filtration to prevent water damage to cargos.

They had also learned that the wooden layers that had been broken through were part of the booby trap. Had Vaughn, McGinnis, and Smith, as well as later diggers, paralleled the Money Pit shaft and then dug in from the side, they probably would have reached the treasure. However, they unwittingly broke the seals, allowing the seawater to flood the pit.

What this demonstrated to all was that whoever had built the Money Pit had a good engineering background. The booby trap was ingeniously designed and worked flawlessly. The size of the operation—creating the artificial beach, digging the drainage system, and sealing it with the wooden "corks"—meant the treasure was extremely valuable. The labor that went into the creation of the Money Pit indicated it was designed to protect something of extreme value for a long period of time.

ANOTHER ASSAULT ON THE MONEY PIT

Nothing more happened during the next eleven years. Smith eventually sold his property on the island, including the Money Pit lot, to Anthony Graves. Apparently Graves found his treasure by allowing others to dig for it on his property.

Next came the Oak Island Association on April 3, 1861, which had the expressed purpose of excavating Oak Island. Some of those who had participated in the old Truro Company were now members of the new association.

They hired a large labor force and gave them the job of reopening the pit. In the decade since the last attempt to recover the treasure, the sides had fallen in. They bailed out the water and dug down to the 88-foot level. There they ran into muddy clay and—believing that it was blocking, or plugging, the water trap—left it in place.

They moved to the west about eighteen feet and began to dig another shaft. When they reached down 118 feet, they began to tunnel toward the Money Pit. They created a tunnel four feet high and three feet wide, hoping to dig into the vault where the treasure was hidden. Up to that point, they had avoided problems with water.

They entered the Money Pit below the platform at 105 feet that had been discovered by the boring operation eleven years earlier. Then, according to Jothan McCully, they "unwisely" dug through the Money Pit to the east. Water began to seep into the pit again. Before long the new shaft was filled and more water was seeping into the Money Pit shaft. Three days of bailing failed to lower the water level. They had tripped the booby trap they had worked so hard to avoid.

This time they weren't going to be defeated by the water. A new bailing operation was begun using dozens of men and horses and they succeeded in nearly draining all the water from the pit. When they finished, they discovered the tunnel leading from their new shaft to the Money Pit was choked with wet clay. Two men were sent down to clear it.

They had removed about half of the obstructing debris when they heard a crash from inside the Money Pit. They had barely made it out of the new pit when another rush of soupy mud poured in.

Other debris was also found during this period. In the September 1861 *Nova Scotian*, one of the diggers, identified only as Patrick, reported that "while the water was hindered by this earth from coming through we took out part of the earth and wood. The wood was stained black with age; it was cut, hewn, chamfered, sawn and bored, according to the purpose for which it was needed. We also took out part of a keg." This material would later provide clues about the actual age of the Money Pit.

Once some of the mud between the west pit and the Money Pit had been cleared, both pits began to flood again, so bailing operations were resumed. But McCully reported that, ". . . on clearing the tunnel again, another crash was heard in the Money Pit which [we] supposed to be the upper platform falling and immediately the bottom of the Money Pit to about 102 feet measuring from the level of the ground to the top. It had been cleared out previously down to 88 feet. Immediately after, the cribbing [walls] of the Money Pit commencing at the bottom, fell in plank after plank until there was only about 30 feet of the upper cribbing. On Monday the top fell in, leaving the old Money Pit a complete mass of ruins."

The platform that had held the two treasure boxes found by the boring operation had apparently fallen fourteen feet and now rested at the 119-foot level. The digging operation had tripped another of the ingenious booby traps. It prevented the operation from recovering any of the treasure at that moment.

THE FIRST RECORDED DEATH IN THE MONEY PIT

The Association raised an additional two thousand dollars to purchase a steam powered pump. Before they had made much progress, the boiler exploded, shutting down the operation for the year.

During this accident, one man was apparently killed by the boiling water. None of the members of the Association mention the fact, but in an essay written some seven years later, E. H. Owen reported the death.

In 1862, the Association returned to Oak Island and began the work all over again. They dug another shaft near the Money Pit reaching down 107 feet. The Money Pit was then cleaned and the sides recribbed to 103 feet. Water began to seep in and, at 103 feet, it began to flow at a rate faster than the pump could handle it.

But the major problem was that the Association was now broke. They set out to raise additional capital, but had little luck.

The additional amount of money raised was so small that it couldn't begin to pay to solve the problems that the Association faced.

To stop the flow of water from Smith's Cove, they wanted to build another cofferdam, but lacked the money to do the job right. Instead they attempted to plug the drains that had been found at low tide. This slowed the rate of the water, but the plugs soon washed away and the flow returned to its original rate.

Work again stopped as the Association attempted to raise money. In August 1863, operations resumed with workmen digging additional tunnels. More pumps were brought in. In 1864, they found the source of the water on the eastern side. Rocks about twice the size of a human head were forced out into the pit. Having found the opening of the booby trap inside the Money Pit, the workers were unable to plug it. Water poured in and all the pumps they had did little to reduce the water level.

The Association was now completely out of money. To make matters worse, mining engineers, concerned about the erosion caused by the constant flow of seawater, declared the pit unsafe. That finished the Oak Island Association.

ANOTHER COMPANY TAKES OVER THE OPERATION

A new company, the Oak Island Contract Company, was formed; it attempted to attract investors, but failed. They estimated they needed about six thousand dollars, but couldn't raise it and abandoned their efforts.

A year later, in May 1866, the Oak Island Eldorado Company was formed. The officers were the same as those in the Contract Company. They succeeded in raising about four thousand dollars, part of which would be used to build a larger, stronger cofferdam. With the sea held at bay, they believed they would be able to recover the hidden wealth.

Although they did build the cofferdam, it was soon destroyed by the Atlantic Ocean. It had done nothing to reduce the rate of water flow into the Money Pit.

With that, the Eldorado Company returned to the island and began drilling operations. This time, however, they used a casing about three inches in diameter. That was significant because it ensured that what was brought up came from deep in the pit, rather than something that might have fallen in at a later date.

They managed to reach depths of 150 feet, finding wood chips, coconut fiber, and charcoal. More water was struck at 140 feet, then soft clay and fine sand.

They did sink a couple of other test holes, but nothing of interest was found. There are also reports that they tried to dig another shaft 175 feet from the Money Pit but no documentation has been found to confirm this. By 1867, they had run out of money and ideas. The corporation was dissolved.

QUARTER OF A CENTURY BREAK

That ended the attempts to recover the treasure for about twenty-five years. In 1893, Frederick Blair formed the Oak Island Treasure Company. One of Blair's accomplishments was a collection of all documentation and an oral history of all the searches that had preceded his. He interviewed many of those who had been involved in earlier attempts to get at the treasure. Blair produced a prospectus, with the help of Adams Tupper, to outline what was known.

The prospectus said:

> It can be proven:
>
> That a shaft about 13 feet in diameter and 100 feet deep was sunk on Oak Island in Mahone Bay, Nova Scotia, before the memory of any now living.
>
> That this shaft was connected by an underground tunnel with the open ocean, about 365 feet distant.
>
> That at the bottom of this shaft were placed large wooden boxes in which were precious metals and jewels.
>
> That many attempts have been made, without success, to obtain this treasure.
>
> That it is reasonably certain the treasure is large, because so great trouble would never have been taken to conceal any small sum.
>
> That it is now entirely feasible to thoroughly explore this shaft and recover the treasure still located therein.

The company planned to raise about sixty thousand dollars for the search. They would use the money to secure the treasure rights and lease the land. The remainder of the shares would stay in the company's safe, to be sold as needed for supplies and payroll. The plans were published and in a short time they had sold enough of the shares to begin their work.

One of the things that made Blair's plan better than those before his was a piece of information he had that his predecessors didn't. Sophia Sellers, daughter of Anthony Graves and wife of Henry, had been plowing when the earth in the field caved in under her team. A hole, six feet in diameter and ten feet deep, had opened under her. Blair noticed that this hole was about 350 feet east of the Money Pit and over what many suspected was the route of the water trap. With that knowledge, he hoped to defeat the hazard.

The task was to explore the cave-in site and then excavate it. They believed that the builders of the Money Pit had hidden a gate of some kind that would allow them to stop the flow of water so they could get at the treasure when they were ready to recover it. However, after digging down to fifty-five feet, the water began to pour in and no amount of bailing would lower it. They abandoned that aspect of their quest.

Another shaft was begun, away from the original Money Pit, but once again water was encountered. Once again, the rate of flow was such that the pumps could not overcome it. And once again the project was abandoned.

By now the whole area around the original Money Pit had been dug up. Several different companies had sunk shafts near the pit, trying to tunnel into it. The whole countryside around the pit was riddled with shafts and tunnels and old excavations. All this time water was flowing from Smith's Cove, under the island and directly into the area to keep workers out. The site was becoming dangerous.

Beginning in 1896, the men began another attempt to excavate. Other companies that had followed the Oak Island Treasure Company filled in some of the pits they had dug. And the original pit, created after the last boring exploration, had been filled in as well. The new task was to excavate the pit and try to keep the water out using their new pumps.

THE MONEY PIT CLAIMS A SECOND VICTIM

On March 26, 1897, Maynard Kaiser was being raised by rope to the top of one of the pits when the rope slipped from the pulley. He plunged back into the pit and was killed. That convinced the other workers that there was some kind of ghostly guardian of the treasure who killed Kaiser as a warning.

After the executives of the latest treasure hunting company convinced the men they could continue work without fear of ghosts, they reached a depth of 110 feet. The pumps were keeping the pit clear of water. They noticed that one of the old tunnels dug in the 1860s was responsible for the water filling the Money Pit. They explored the tunnel and found another leading to a large pit from which the water was coming. Blair realized that this was the original Money Pit. They had just spent a great deal of time, effort, and money excavating the wrong shaft.

They began to excavate the real Money Pit. They reached 111 feet when they came to a new tunnel that was two and a half feet wide on the east side. The water was pouring through it with such force that the men realized they'd never be able to block it. In fact, water was pouring through so fast that it filled the Money Pit and all the other shafts to the tide level. They'd have to stop the flow at the other source if they planned to block it at all.

WHO OWNED THE TREASURE?

As they retreated to Halifax to devise an attack plan, another problem arose. The legal ownership of any treasure recovered was in dispute. English law gave the rights to the crown, allowing the monarch to reassign a percentage to the discoverer. However, it was not required for the finder to receive anything except the thanks of the crown. In other words, the crown could take all the treasure without any compensation to those who had actually found it.

Earlier companies operated under a treasure license granted by the crown and took their chances. If the reigning monarch was generous, they would be amply rewarded. That situation changed in 1867 when the Dominion of Canada was created by the British North America Act of 1867.

Under the new law, the province had the authority over any treasure. Blair petitioned the Nova Scotian government. An agreement was reached giving two percent of the treasure to the government and dividing the rest among the various shareholders and company officials once the treasure had been recovered.

With all the legal problems finally resolved, they went back to work, deciding to dynamite the drains at Smith's Cove and plug them there. That should stop the flow of water and allow them the chance to dig down to the treasure.

The third hole they dug in Smith's Cove broke through into a shaft filled with water. Convinced they had found the channel through which the water filled the pit, they crammed it with dynamite, filled it in, and then set off the charge. Water and debris flew a hundred-feet into the air. The water in the Money Pit boiled with activity.

They were convinced they had succeeded where others had failed, yet the pumps could barely keep up with the flow. With the pumps working twenty-four hours a day, they were able to hold the water at the hundred-foot level. The company erected a platform and spent the rest of the summer of 1897 boring exploratory holes.

The major find was a cement vault about 150 feet down. Inside the vault there seemed to be a chest filled with loose metal. Continuing the operation, they discovered an iron plate at 171 feet. They were unable to bore through that.

Analysis of the recovered fillings confirmed the belief that there were iron plates in the pit. Analysis also revealed that there was a concrete vault, obviously something that had been created by human hands.

By the fall of 1897, the directors of the company were more convinced than ever that they were digging for a huge treasure. They decided to dig two additional pits to 180 feet, away from the original site, and then tunnel over. They wanted to come up under the iron plate.

Water again defeated them. One shaft reached only 70 feet before the water burst through from one of the other tunnels. The second shaft reached 160 feet before water drove them out. Pumping failed to reduce the level of the water and the effort had to be abandoned.

The next summer, they decided to again plug the drainage system in Smith's Cove. To precisely locate the drains, they decided to throw dye into the Money Pit. By pumping water into the pit, they hoped to backwash the system. That would force the dye through it, identifying the specific drain sites and allowing them to be plugged.

They were horrified when the plan worked all too well. Dye showed up in Smith's Cove, as they had expected. But it also appeared on the south side of the island in what is called South Shore Cove. Dynamiting the drains in Smith's Cove, even if successful, would do little to stop the flow of water.

They spent the next two years digging additional shafts, trying to defeat the water booby traps. But each shaft soon filled with water. They ran into lateral tunnels that other searchers dug the century before they began the new work. Blair and his associates figured that the water flowing into the pit had to come from more than the two identified sources but he couldn't prove it.

By 1900, the whole Oak Island Treasure Company was about to sink. A new prospectus was written and some additional capital brought in. They dug another shaft but it, too, flooded, driving out the workers. Additional exploratory holes were bored but produced no interesting results. The company was broke and unable to continue. The Oak Island Treasure Company finally gave up.

Blair, however, was caught under the spell of Oak Island. Spending his own money, he retained his lease on the Money Pit acreage. And he kept the treasure license from Nova Scotia in force. Blair was convinced that the Oak Island Money Pit could be defeated and he was going to do it.

In 1909, Henry L. Bowdoin, who had been hearing about the Money Pit for years, joined forces with Blair. Bowdoin was convinced that with modern equipment and divers, it would be a relatively simple task to recover the treasure. In April 1909, he formed the Old Gold Salvage and Wrecking Company in New York City.

In August 1909, Bowdoin and members of his company sailed from New York to Halifax. On August 27, they arrived on Oak Island and established their headquarters, which they dubbed "Camp Kidd."

After some preliminary work, such as searching for the drains in Smith's Cove and South Shore Cove, they moved their equipment to the Money Pit. Without the 1,000-gallon per-minute pump they had planned to buy but couldn't afford, they couldn't lower the water level at all. They decided to send down the diver.

The diver dropped to about 113 feet. The way was clear to that point, but beyond it, there was wreckage from the many other attempts to reach the treasure. Bowdoin hauled up the diver and then dropped dynamite into the pit to try to clear the way. This was accomplished.

Next, they began to probe the bottom of the pit, boring through it in an attempt to recreate, or corroborate, the findings of the 1897 expedition. Twenty-eight holes were bored, but according to the records kept by Bowdoin, they found nothing to indicate any treasure.

Like the expeditions before him, Bowdoin soon ran out of money. He failed to sell any more shares in his treasure company, even with a prospectus that claimed the reward would be more than ten million dollars for those who were lucky enough to invest.

Over the next few months, Bowdoin exchanged correspondence with Blair. The tone of the letters was less than cordial. Blair accused Bowdoin of being overconfident and undercapitalized. Although Bowdoin wanted to extend their contract, Blair refused, insisting that Bowdoin prove that he had the financing to mount a proper expedition. Bowdoin responded that he would tell the world that the Oak Island treasure was a hoax.

On August 19, 1911, he did just that. In *Collier's* Bowdoin published "Solving the Mystery of Oak Island." He wrote, "My experience proved to me that there is not, and never was, a buried treasure on Oak Island. The Mystery is solved."

Over the next several years there were additional attempts to recover the treasure. Bowdoin's article had not done much to stop the interest in Oak Island. However, none of these attempts made much progress in either learning anything new about the Money Pit or in recovering the treasure hidden in it.

WORK STOPS AGAIN AND THEN STARTS AGAIN

Blair's search for another investor, or group of investors, failed to produce results until 1931. Even then, it wasn't the newspaper articles and advertisements that produced the investor; it was one man's long interest in Oak Island, and the fact that he had been on the platform in 1897 when the drilling operation provided some corroboration for the belief in the treasure.

The malpais in northern New Mexico where Adams said his lost mine could be found. PHOTO BY KEVIN D. RANDLE.

Deep in the malpais, an old lava flow from a long gone volcano, where Adams said he had found the rich placer gold deposit. PHOTO BY KEVIN D. RANDLE.

The malpais, west of Albuquerque and near Interstate 40 in northern New Mexico, locations of the Lost Adams. PHOTO BY KEVIN D. RANDLE.

Various newspaper articles from the early twentieth century reporting on the Lost Adams. PHOTO BY KEVIN D. RANDLE.

The Superstition Mountains, scene of one of the most persistent lost mine legends. PHOTO BY KEVIN D. RANDLE.

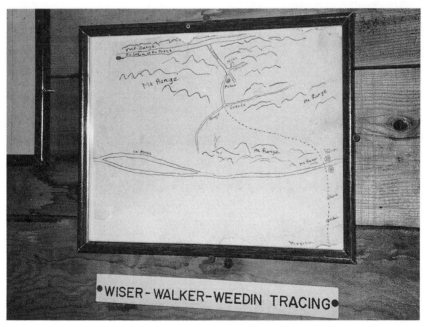

WISER - WALKER - WEEDIN TRACING

One of the many maps that is supposed to lead to the fabulous Lost Dutchman Mine. PHOTO COURTESY OF THE SUPERSTITION MOUNTAIN MUSEUM, APACHE JUNCTION (GOLDFIELD), AZ; PHOTO BY KEVIN D. RANDLE.

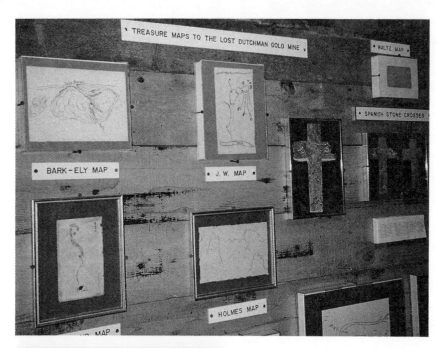

Some of the many of the maps that have been used in the search for the Lost Dutchman Mine (*this page and opposite, top right*).

PHOTOS COURTESY OF THE SUPERSTITION MOUNTAIN MUSEUM, APACHE JUNCTION (GOLDFIELD), AZ; PHOTO BY KEVIN D. RANDLE.

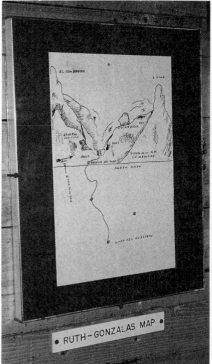

Weaver's Needle, often reported as the starting point for all searches for the Lost Dutchman Mine. PHOTO BY KEVIN D. RANDLE.

The western side of the Superstition Mountains, where the Lost Dutchman is hidden. PHOTO BY KEVIN D. RANDLE.

Looking at the northern end of the Superstition Mountains not far from Weaver's Needle. PHOTO BY KEVIN D. RANDLE.

The Impact Meteorite Crater outside Odessa, Texas where Ben Sublett lived. Sublett's lost mine war far to the north. PHOTO BY KEVIN D. RANDLE.

Main Street in Hatch, NM. Doc Noss, who claimed to have found a huge treasure in Victorio's Peak, was killed in Hatch in 1949. PHOTO BY KEVIN D. RANDLE.

Looking down at the White Sands Missile Range base from a mountain pass in the Organ Mountains. Father La Rue was supposed to have found a rich gold mine, which is reported to be one of the sources of the gold in Victorio Peak. PHOTO BY KEVIN D. RANDLE.

The San Andres Mountains just north of Las Cruces, NM. Victorio Peak, where Doc Noss claimed to have found a huge treasure, is in this range. PHOTO BY KEVIN D. RANDLE.

William Chappell of Sydney, Nova Scotia, knew that the treasure existed. Since he had been on the crew in 1897, his family's lumber business had expanded and produced huge profits. He decided to use some of the money in another attempt to recover the treasure.

Their first problem was to figure out where to dig. No work had been done for over twenty years. The area was riddled with holes and shafts dug by those trying to recover the treasure. Chappell finally settled on a site and began his operation. When Blair visited the island, he told Chappell that he was digging in the wrong place.

Chappell decided to dig a large shaft around the Money Pit. With the help of an electric pump, he kept his new shaft relatively dry. As they dug, they found old tools and an anchor fluke. They reached a depth that no one else had managed, but then things turned to the worse. First, so many shafts had been sunk, and so much water had been forced in and pumped out, that the ground had turned into a soup. The soft earth began caving in. They also found what might have been the mouth of the drain from South Shore Cove. They couldn't plug it, but that didn't matter. The pump was up to the task of keeping the water out of the shaft.

By the end of the summer, they had spent forty thousand dollars and accomplished very little. They shut down the operation for the season, believing they would come back the next year to finish it. That, however, didn't work out.

The next complication was created by a dozen people. Sophia Sellers, who owned the Money Pit, died, and her heirs were each requiring a huge sum before consenting to further operations.

In the summer of 1932, the heirs allowed another party to begin. Blair still held the treasure trove rights so that he would be involved in the recovery if there was one. That new operation was of little value and failed to produce any results.

In 1933, another man, Thomas Nixon, began his work on Oak Island. He grossly misrepresented himself and did little more than drill a number of holes. In his report, he claimed to have confirmed some of the items from the 1897 diggings, but that was all. He wanted Blair to extend his search contract and when Blair refused, Nixon threatened to sue.

Blair was no longer interested in Nixon and his tales. He had found another investor, Gilbert Hedden, from New Jersey. His family had sold a business, leaving Hedden with the financial resources to pursue his dream of solving the riddle of Oak Island. Hedden told Blair that he was prepared to spend $100,000 to recover the treasure.

In the beginning, the first of the companies formed had invested only four to six thousand dollars, hired dozens of men, and spent months on the island. Now, about a hundred years later, with the mystery unsolved and the treasure still in the ground, the stakes were considerably higher. Of course technology might overcome the booby traps that sheer determination couldn't.

Blair tried to arrange for the various rights, but the Sellers heirs refused to allow him to dig. They had learned that a millionaire from the United States wanted to dig and they wanted $5,500 for the land. That was ten times what it was worth, unless, of course, there was a treasure in the pit. Then it could be worth, literally, millions of dollars.

Blair attempted an end run by having legislation introduced that would allow the holding of a treasure trove license to dig on land owned by someone else. If the two parties couldn't reach an agreement, then arbitration would settle the matter. The law was not enacted.

But that made no difference. Hedden finally caved in and paid five thousand dollars for the eastern end of the island. But it was too late in the season to begin any new operations. Another year had been lost.

In 1936, Hedden was finally ready. Rather than attack the Money Pit, he decided to drain the pit dug by Chappell and explore the area around it. Using a huge pump, he was able to drain the Chappell pit, the cave-in pit, and several of the other shafts dug by earlier expeditions. The operations failed to recover the treasure.

There was an important discovery, however. Hedden, searching the island, found a number of rocks, some arranged in a curious triangular shape that seemed related to the construction of the Money Pit. There were even rumors that these artifacts were related to a map included in a book about Captain Kidd. Those connections seem to have been eliminated by later investigations, so the connection to Kidd is tenuous at best. However, the stones found on Oak Island did prove that those who built the Money Pit understood engineering, astronomy, and navigation. That would seem to rule out many of the theories about who hid the treasure there.

Hedden spent a great deal of time and effort chasing the strange map from the book about Kidd. When he discovered that the map was the figment of the writer's imagination, his enthusiasm for the search might have evaporated. At any rate, when the time came for Hedden to renew his agreement with Blair, Hedden let it lapse. (Of course the fact that Hedden was in trouble with the IRS might also have contributed to his decision.)

When Hedden bowed out in 1938, Erwin H. Hamilton, a mechanical engineering professor at New York University, was ready to step in. In fact, he had approached Blair a couple of years earlier only to be told that Hedden owned the land and had the rights to dig. But then the way was cleared in 1938 for Hamilton to take over the operation.

Hamilton conducted a number of tests, including another one using dye. He mapped the various tunnels dug under the island and planned his new assault. However, the Second World War started and prevented Hamilton from proceeding.

From that point on and through the 1940s, a number of different men tried to recover the treasure. Some of the attempts were little more than negotiations, which fell apart as the participants failed to agree on who would get how much of the treasure. The property on which the Money Pit was located was sold by Hedden, fell back into his hands, and was sold again. Nothing of importance was accomplished although there were some interesting developments. President Roosevelt, for example, maintained a correspondence with a number of men involved in the search and even made plans to visit Oak Island.

Work on Oak Island would not begin again until the mid-1950s. George Greene, an oil man from Texas, applied to Chappell, who now owned the property, for permission to drill. He sank a number of holes, found a huge void below 140 feet, and pumped tens of thousands of gallons of water into it. The water disappeared, flowing out. Greene promised to return the next year but didn't. He was murdered in 1962. That had nothing to do with Oak Island.

THE MONEY PIT CLAIMS ADDITIONAL VICTIMS

Nothing more was accomplished until 1959 when Bob Restall moved to the island. He had fallen under the spell during a chance visit several years earlier. Although his financing was always small, his passion ran high. With his family—wife, Mildred, and his sons—he moved to the island, living in a couple of shacks that had no indoor plumbing, running water, and for the first few years, no electricity.

Without the large financing that was available to some of the corporations and syndicates that had been formed over the years, Restall couldn't rent heavy equipment. The search was reduced to what it had been about 150 years earlier—picks and shovels and backbreaking manual labor.

Restall tried to block the flood tunnel from Smith's Cove, pouring cement into the drains, but that failed. He tried to locate the main tunnel to block it and failed.

Restall had other problems as well. His lease on the treasure hunting operation was from year to year. Chappell was always bringing around potential investors and introducing them to Restall. They would discuss the treasure and theories about it. Restall was convinced there was thirty million dollars buried in the Money Pit. He based that on the original stone that had been translated to say that two million pounds was hidden. Restall converted the two million pounds to dollars, basing the calculation on the rate of exchange in the late eighteenth century.

On August 17, 1965, Restall's treasure hunt ended. Restall was working in what was called the Hedden shaft and was either looking into it, or had begun to climb down into it, when he fell. His son, seeing his father in the water, started to climb down to help him. He slipped from the ladder.

Karl Graeser, who was visiting the island with an eye to beginning his own hunt, arrived at the scene, saw both Restalls in the hole, and started down to rescue them. Behind him was Virgil Hiltz, a teenager hired by Restall. Both of them fell victim as well. Andy DeMont, another teenager working for Restall, tried to rescue them all.

Others who were vacationing or visiting the island ran to help. One of them was a firefighter, Edward White. He realized that some kind of gas had seeped into the pit. He tied a rope around his waist and was lowered into the water. He found

DeMont and tied a rope around him. He tried to find the others, but couldn't. As he was losing consciousness, he was hauled out.

White and DeMont survived. The bodies of the other four were eventually recovered. No one knows exactly what happened and there are debates about the gas that had seeped into the pit. Whatever it was, it was deadly and the death toll climbed by four.

But almost before the bodies were buried, Chappell was back with another investor, Bob Dunfield. He brought in bulldozers, scraped the area around the Money Pit clear, and shoved tons of dirt into Smith's Cove. That muddied the water there, but the water flooding the Pit was clear. Dunfield believed that he had finally succeeded in blocking the drains from Smith's Cove. That left one other tunnel flooding the pit.

Dunfield built a causeway from the island to the mainland so that he could bring over additional heavy equipment. He used that equipment to dig up much of the area. He drilled additional holes confirming the results of other such tests and found a void under the island that he believed to be a natural formation.

Equipment breakdowns, the hostility of the locals, and lousy weather forced him to return home. He wanted to buy the island, but Chappell wanted $100,000. Dunfield couldn't raise the money, or felt the price was out of line. Whatever the reason, he lost interest in the project although he did believe there was treasure in the Money Pit.

For the next several years, a variety of people became interested in the Money Pit. Many of these people would later combine to form the Oak Island Exploration Company. They would have a ten million dollar plan to recover the treasure. With the equipment available, and with the expanding and growing technology, it was believed they could overwhelm the booby traps and the genius of the designer.

THE BEGINNINGS OF THE LAST ASSAULT

In 1968, Dan Blankenship and a Montreal businessman, David Tobias, formed a partnership to recover the treasure. Both men had been interested for a number of years. They formed the Triton Alliance Ltd.

In 1971, one of the small bore holes was enlarged, encased in steel, and named Borehole 10X. The idea was to put a video camera down, into the void under the island. Blankenship, watching the screen, saw something strange. He called over others and asked what they saw. To a man, they said that a severed human hand floated, suspended, in the murky water.

Another probe picked up what looked to be three chests and one clearly defined handle. They also saw various tools, spikes, and logs. Finally they saw a human body, with the skin and hair mostly intact, slumped against a wall. Pathologists have suggested that a body submerged in salt water, in an airless environment, might be preserved. It would be the same as pickling it in brine.

With Borehole 10X enlarged to the point where a man could climb down, exploration at the bottom was conducted. Because the end of the shaft was underwater, divers were lowered. The first diver reported a strong current as he exited the borehole into the chamber that had been found. It was suspected this was caused by the flood tunnels. More earth was pushed into Smith's Cove, and on a second dive, the current was gone.

Borehole 10X was 230 feet deep. The metal casing was forced down to 180 feet. The remainder of the hole was through the natural rock and soil of Oak Island. At 230 feet, the borehole ended in a void where the television camera recorded the hand, body, and other items.

The water was filled with debris, and as the diver rubbed against the walls of the chamber, the rock crumbled, filling the water with a chalky substance. Given the depth, the closed quarters, and the debris in the water, the divers couldn't see much. Blankenship, who made several dives himself, reported that it would be suicide to move away from the bottom of the borehole.

On a dive in November 1976, Blankenship heard a deep rumbling somewhere above him. He demanded to be hauled out as fast as possible. As he looked down, the casing of Borehole 10X collapsed. Later, Blankenship, checking the damage to the borehole, found solid ground at the 73-foot level. Drilling found the twisted remains of the borehole casing at 90 feet.

There were attempts to recreate Borehole 10X, but mechanical problems and funding hindered the completion of the project. When they continued to work, pushing the hole deeper into the island. When they reached 167 feet, the project, which had yielded nothing of significance, was abandoned.

Legal maneuverings, disputes over the ownership of part of the island, and fights about the use of the causeway, slowed the hunt for a number of years. All the time, some work was being accomplished, but the legal maneuvers caused troubles with financing for the projects. Those with the money didn't want to jeopardize their capital until the legal matters were completely settled.

THE BIG DIG

Tobias, Blankenship, and the Triton Alliance planned a big dig on Oak Island. Using ten million dollars, they would defeat the booby traps and recover whatever was hidden in the depths. Plans called for a huge shaft over the Money Pit with pumps that could keep the seawater out. The new shaft would be large enough to encompass all the earlier workings so the exact location of the original pit, somewhat in dispute, was not a problem.

Tobias had found twenty underwriters and believed that the financing was in place. By now they were talking of a treasure worth between a hundred million and several billion dollars. He refused to guess what might be hidden, but was sure that it was extremely valuable.

The Stock Market crash of 1987 left many of the speculators scared. They withdrew their support. But Tobias came up with a new plan. He would sell the television rights to the big dig, broadcasting a special similar to *The Mystery of Al Capone's Vault*.

As of 1995, the big dig has not taken place. The Triton Alliance has had to postpone their plans a number of times. Some of it has had to do with financing, but part of it has to do with the credibility of the story. After all, there is no solid proof that anything of value is in the Money Pit.

Theories about it abound. Some believe it is pirate gold, some believe it was treasure from Europe, some believe it is the lost original manuscripts of William Shakespeare, and some are convinced it is nothing more than an elaborate hoax. A few think that treasure was there once, but was removed, probably by the original designer.

Evidence pulled up during the many test drillings have produced some interesting results. Tobias had some of the material—the coconut husk, samples of wood recovered at the bottom of the pit, and iron spikes—analyzed. According to the National Museum of Natural Sciences, the spikes had probably been forged prior to 1790. The wood was carbon dated to 1575, plus or minus 85 years. That means the treasure could have been put down there as early as 1490 or as late as 1650. In other words, the Money Pit had been dug at least 150 years before it was found.

Clearly the evidence—from the stone triangle found in the summer of 1965 and the cofferdam erected in Smith's Cove, to stones that were carved and scattered on the island—shows a presence there. The Money Pit is a worked area, constructed for some purpose. That is not in dispute. And it could have been contructed two years before Columbus set sail for the New World. More likely, it was built some time after that, but the point is, it predates 1795 by decades.

So, is there a treasure? It seems unlikely that someone would invest the time and effort to construct the pit without putting something valuable at the bottom. Whoever built it would have been able to recover that treasure if he had decided to do so. And, if it had been recovered, wouldn't they have left an open hole rather than filling it in and resetting the booby traps? In other words, the best theory is that whoever built the Money Pit, put in the treasure, and then, for whatever reason, was unable to get back to retrieve it.

However, one of the theories is that the Money Pit itself is a red herring. Those who built it dug a side tunnel, or two or three from the main shaft, and used these tunnels to hide their treasure. A hundred yards, two hundred from the main pit, closer to the ground, was the treasure. The Money Pit was then filled in with the booby traps set. If the original owner of the treasure returned, he could dig down thirty or forty feet, out the proper distance from the main pit, recover his loot, and be gone. The main shaft would be undisturbed. And anyone who found the island would dig up the Money Pit assuming, incorrectly, that the treasure had to be at the bottom of it.

The treasure then, could be somewhere else on the island, or it could be gone, recovered long before the pit was found in 1795. There have been indications of loose metal held in chests, but no one has recovered the chests. There are the three gold links brought up during one of the drilling operations. So there is an indication that something was buried and that it is still there.

Oak Island is unique in the field of treasure hunting. Everyone knows where the treasure is. At the bottom of the pit. Modern technology should be able to defeat the booby traps, but financing, legal squabbles, and bad luck have prevented that. Any archaeological benefits have probably been destroyed by all those who dug before. The huge earth-moving machines that plow up tons of dirt certainly could have destroyed any archaeological evidence. They did ruin the stone triangle, and some of the carved stones near Smith's Cove have disappeared.

It seems that we'll have the answers in just a few years. When the story began in 1795 the technology to recover the treasure didn't exist. The booby traps were big and clever enough to prevent the boys from finding anything. It could have been recovered fifty or a hundred years ago if the work had been well planned and sufficient financing had been in place. Those problems are being resolved. Once they are, it seems that the Triton Alliance, or any of the treasure hunters that follow them, will finally solve the puzzle. The only downside will be if the treasure is so small that it doesn't cover the expense of the search.

7

VICTORIO PEAK

—

NEW MEXICO

Like the treasure stories from Oak Island, the exact location of this treasure trove is well known. It is buried in a cave in the San Andres Mountains north of Las Cruces, New Mexico on what is now part of the Army's White Sands Missile Range. The mountain is known as Victorio Peak, though one of the major books about the hidden treasure refers to the location as Victoria's Peak.

There had been rumors of a large gold supply in the area for hundreds of years. A Jesuit priest, unhappy with the situation in old Mexico at the end of the eighteenth century, and having heard tales of great wealth in the arid north, organized his own expedition. Father La Rue heard the story of vast wealth from a dying soldier. La Rue believed that the gold was there for the taking. If his expedition was formed only with those from his personal circle of friends, then he could control any wealth he found and wouldn't have to share it with the church in Rome.

The tale is that La Rue, after traveling into what is now southern New Mexico, set up his operation in the Organ Mountains

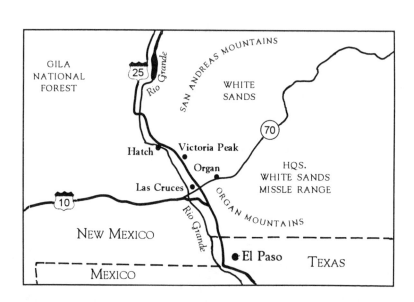

GILA NATIONAL FOREST

25

Rio Grande

SAN ANDREAS MOUNTAINS

WHITE SANDS

70

Hatch · Victoria Peak ·

Organ ·

Las Cruces ·

10

ORGAN MOUNTAINS

HQS. WHITE SANDS MISSLE RANGE

NEW MEXICO

Rio Grande

MEXICO

· El Paso TEXAS

to the east of present day Las Cruces. For two years he extracted gold from the mountains, stockpiling it.

It seems that La Rue wanted nothing more than to be left alone to teach the word of Christ, and to mine the gold. But that wasn't to be. Apparently word leaked into Mexico that La Rue had set up his own little empire and that he was extracting a mountain of gold. Nothing stirred the fires of the Spanish like tales of gold. An armed expedition was sent north to find the truth.

La Rue discovered the expedition as it was nearing his outpost. To prevent the gold from falling into the hands of those he hated, La Rue hid all evidence of the mining, hid the gold he had refined, and sealed the cave where it was stored. Although the historical facts seem to suggest he was in the Organ Mountains between present day Las Cruces and Alamogordo, apparently his mining operation was deep in the San Andres Mountains north of Las Cruces. It was here, according to legend, that the treasure was concealed.

The expedition from Mexico arrived and attacked. La Rue was captured, tortured, and ordered repeatedly to reveal his secret. La Rue refused. During the process, La Rue died.

Others of his band were captured, but none revealed the location of the treasure. The soldiers searched the area, but could find no clues. They returned to Mexico empty-handed. Some thought that given the time they would be able to find the treasure. No one ever returned to search for it.

Stories of lost mines and treasure are told throughout the Southwest. The Spanish had searched the area for decades, looking for gold. They did find and work mines in the vicinity. Records show that only a fraction of the treasure ever reached Spain. Some was lost due to shipwreck. Other parties were attacked and killed by Indians before they could reach the ships. And some, realizing they couldn't carry all their treasure away, hid it to be retrieved later.

The story of La Rue, and of the vast stores in Victorio Peak, seems to have more life than most. For nearly fifty years it has been the subject of an ongoing battle between those who found it—those who believe they have a claim to it—and the United States Army at the White Sands Missile Range.

DOC NOSS AND THE CAVE OF TREASURE

Milton Ernest "Doc" Noss, who said he found a vast treasure in Victorio's Peak, claimed to be two-thirds Cheyenne. He was born in Oklahoma and had worked various jobs in the Southwest. It is unclear if he ever claimed to hold a medical degree but he did work to cure the foot ailments of many locals. Later, some would assume that he was a medical man, but no record exists to prove this.

In 1937, Noss and his wife Ova were residents of New Mexico, living in the vicinity of Hatch. He spent time hunting or prospecting in the area around Victorio Peak. During one such outing he was caught by a cold, spring storm and sought shelter under an outcropping of rock near the summit of the mountain.

It was a place that apparently had been used for centuries by other hunters. Noss saw evidence of early inhabitants, but didn't know if they had lived there long, or merely used it as a temporary shelter. Sitting there, waiting for the rain to stop, he noticed a stone that looked as if it had been worked in some fashion. Noss reached down, couldn't budge it, and then began digging around the edges of it. After all, he had nothing better to do on that cold, rainy afternoon. When he could work his hands under it, he lifted it clear and found a shaft that descended into darkness.

Noss was curious about the shaft, but it was too late in the day to do anything about it. Besides, he was not equipped to make any sort of reconnaissance. The next day he returned with a flashlight, rope, and a canvas bag. Even with these preparations he was unable to probe much of the shaft, but he saw enough to interest him in exploring further.

In the weeks to follow, Noss returned to the site whenever possible. He reached the bottom of the shaft, but his flashlight was not adequate for the task; its beam was too dim to chase away the gloom. Noss eventually found an underground stream but couldn't see the bank on the other side or how deep it was. He was afraid to try to cross it.

Finally, Noss crossed the stream, while above him Ova waited for his return, boiling coffee and making sandwiches. Hours later, he finally emerged from the shaft. He held out his canvas sack, now stuffed with something heavy. He tossed a black bar on the ground near the fire, thinking it was nothing more important than iron.

Years later, while giving a deposition about the first entry into the cave, Ova Noss would claim that she was the one who first scraped at the iron bar and discovered that it was gold. In the original story, Noss said that he had discovered that the bar was gold and not iron while sitting around the fire. It makes no difference now who made the discovery.

Noss would tell Ova there were stacks of the bars in the cavern. He also said that he found uncut jewels, including rubies, coins, religious artifacts such as a gold Virgin Mary statue, and other manufactured items including swords. There were also trunks with clothes and Wells Fargo chests. Later, the wealth in the cave was calculated to be worth more than two billion dollars. No matter what the estimate, it was clear that Noss was telling his wife they had found a substantial treasure, much of it in gold bullion.

Noss was clever enough to realize that any news of the find would fill the area with treasure hunters, prospectors, and con men. Also, in 1937, there was a law that made it illegal for private citizens to own gold bullion. If word got out, they might have to go to jail, and the government would take the treasure leaving them with nothing. Noss told his wife that they must not mention the gold to anyone.

Noss, however, didn't live up to his own orders. He showed the gold bar to a friend in Hot Springs (later Truth or Consequences, NM). When asked if he had found it in the Caballo Mountains, Noss said, "That's right."

It wasn't long before the Caballos were filled with prospectors. Noss was delighted with the results. The Caballos were miles from the actual site on Victorio Peak.

As far as Noss was concerned, he had found a huge treasure that would make him rich. It was difficult to get at the gold and drag it out; some of the bars weighed eighty pounds. Still, he hauled many bars out. Accounts vary, some suggesting that he carried several hundred bars from out of the cave. He then hid those in various locations, hoping to find a way to make money off the gold.

Here is a real dilemma for those accepting the Noss story. He had found wealth of such magnitude that it would eclipse that of everyone except the very rich. There were gold coins and jewels, according to Noss, which could have been sold to collectors without violating the laws. There were legal means of disposing of the wealth, but Noss never followed any of those. Apparently he never bothered to consult with anyone who could tell him the truth. Instead, he tried to enlist investors to help him recover his treasure. He was willing to share it if he could get his hands on it all.

He also complained that the passage to the treasure cave was so narrow at one point that he had to crawl forward carefully, his shoulders scraping the rough stone walls. In 1939, he hired another man, an expert with explosives named Montgomery, to widen the passage with dynamite. Montgomery used too much explosive and collapsed the tunnel, filling it with debris. Access to the treasure room was now impossible by the original route.

GOLD BARS AND TALES OF TREASURE

Now the treasure was just beyond his reach. He knew it was there because he had seen it repeatedly, but he couldn't get to it. There are conflicting accounts, but it seems that no one, other than Noss, ever saw the gold in the cave. He did show metal bars to others, and in her deposition, Ova Noss would say that she had seen a large number of bars that she identified as gold but that she had not seen the gold in the cave.

About ten years after he found the gold, Noss claimed he traveled to the Denver mint in an attempt to sell some of it to the government. Noss was vague about where he had gotten the gold, so officials at the mint confiscated it, supplying him with a receipt saying they had $90,000 in gold taken from him. Noss claimed the receipt was in a strong box. Upon his death, a search for the receipt failed to find it. Ova Noss even traveled to Denver, but mint officials found no record of Noss being there or turning over anything to them.

There are those who claim this is just another example of the government covering up. However, it was Noss who told the story and it was Noss who claimed to have a receipt to prove his claim. Neither he nor family members were ever able to produce that receipt, according to Ova Noss's attorney, Phil Koury. Later, Gene Ballinger, writing in *The Courier* (the Hatch, NM newspaper) said that the receipt was in the possession of the Ova Noss Family Partnership. If the receipt exists, it would go a long way toward documenting Doc Noss's claim of finding treasure. It would have provided some proof for the Army that the treasure existed after matters deteriorated between the Noss family and the U.S. Army at White Sands a decade later.

Noss spent years attempting to gather capital to reopen the treasure cave. He showed treasure in various forms to various people. In an affidavit contained at the Land Office in Santa Fe, New Mexico, B. D. Lampros claims that he visited Noss and was given a chunk of gold ore that assayed to over $5,000 in gold per ton, which is extremely rich.

Others also presented affidavits about the gold they saw in Noss's possession. Some saw a bar or two, while others were shown ore. Noss apparently carried a great deal of the treasure from the cave, but was never able to successfully sell any of it to finance his recovery operations.

Some time after his discovery, during the Second World War, Noss took off, deserting Ova. In November 1945, Noss was granted a divorce from Ova in Pulaski County, Arkansas. Two years later he married Violet Lena Boles. All of this would complicate ownership of the treasure rights.

During this time, Ova Noss kept the various land applications and mining claims in force, signing and renewing them as necessary. Ova, sometimes with the help of her sons, tried to clean out the shaft that had been ruined in 1939 by Montgomery, the explosives expert. They were unable to clear the passage into the treasure chambers far below.

At the same time, apparently with no permits and therefore no legal rights, Noss was searching Victorio Peak for another entrance into the cave. He believed there had to be one simply because the entrance he had originally discovered would have made it nearly impossible to carry the gold and other treasure into the cave.

CHARLES RYAN AND THE DEATH OF DOC NOSS

In 1948, Noss met Charles Ryan, a Texan involved in drilling operations and oil exploration in West Texas. Noss told Ryan about the treasure and they worked out a deal. Ryan would buy some of the gold from Noss for $25,000. Ryan was to fly into New Mexico where the bars were hidden. Noss would produce them and Ryan would pay for them.

However, when it came time for the exchange, Noss demanded to see the money first. Ryan said that he would not produce the money until Noss produced the gold. According to the story, they drove into Hatch, New Mexico, to a house rented by Ryan. Several people saw Noss run from the house, followed by Ryan who was holding a gun. Ryan fired one shot, apparently into the air, ordering Noss away from a pickup truck. Noss didn't obey and Ryan fired again, hitting Noss in the head. Noss collapsed and died there immediately.

Ryan ordered someone to call the sheriff. When deputies arrived, Ryan was arrested. Ryan told the sheriff that he had fired in self-defense, claiming that he feared for his life. Noss had threatened to kill him and kept a pistol in the glove box of his truck.

During the trial, evidence was presented suggesting that Noss was a violent man. He had bragged that he had killed men before. Because of the many stories that Noss had told about his violent past, Ryan was sure that Noss was going for his pistol. He fired a warning shot but Noss had ignored it.

What was interesting about the trial was the evidence presented about Noss and his background. Ryan had financed Noss, buying him a pickup truck, and traveling to New Mexico in an attempt to obtain the licenses and permits that Ova had kept in force. It also turned out Ryan had bailed Noss out of jail, and paid off a number of bad checks that Noss had written. Altogether Ryan invested about $5,000 in Noss. Ryan also learned, from other sources, that Noss had swindled many other people in New Mexico.

Ryan, called to the stand, told of a plan Noss had devised. He wanted to form a corporation, selling stock in a venture to recover the treasure. Ryan believed they could raise, quickly, something in the neighborhood of $50,000. That would give them capital to operate. Noss, however, suggested that he take $25,000 and Ryan the remaining $25,000. Ryan said that it was the first time he realized that Noss was crooked.

Just prior to the shooting in Hatch, Noss told Ryan that he had a chance to make nearly a quarter of a million dollars selling gold bars to a man from Arizona. To make it all work, Noss needed some seed money from Ryan, who now refused to give it.

It was after that argument, at Ryan's rented house in Hatch, that Noss ran for the truck. According to Ryan, Noss screamed that he would get the money from Ryan, or kill him. Ryan killed Noss instead. The jury believed Ryan and acquitted him.

The trial rarely mentioned the treasure. It did, however, provide additional clues into Noss's background. Noss had claimed to some that he was a doctor by profession. However, he had no formal training in any medical specialty. Searches of hospital records where Noss claimed to be on staff failed to turn up his name. Noss had written a number of bad checks. He had been in and out of jail on rather minor charges. His history was not sterling, which is not to say that the story of the treasure is bogus. It does, however, cast some doubt.

OVA NOSS AND THE U.S. GOVERNMENT

With the death of Doc Noss, Ova became the force behind the attempts to recover the treasure. Others who believed they had a claim began to come forward. One of those was Noss's second wife. Ova dismissed her claim, saying that her divorce from Noss was not legal and therefore his marriage to Violet Noss was not valid. But Violet Noss was inquiring about the legality of the permits held by Ova Noss and was attempting to have them switched over.

Ova's real problem, however, came from the U.S. government and the Army. Not long after Doc Noss was killed, the

Army entered into a lease agreement with Roy Henderson for the land where Victorio Peak is located. Before that, the Gilmore family had lived there. In other words, much of the disputed land belonged, not to the Noss family, but to someone else.

A search of mining records in December 1950 showed no existing mining claims. On November 14, 1951, Public Land Order No. 703 was issued, which withdrew all the White Sands Proving Ground (later the White Sands Missile Range) from prospecting, entry, location, and purchase under the mining laws and reserved their use for the military.

State officials in New Mexico claimed that they leased the surface of the land to the military. The underground wealth, in whatever form it took, belonged to the state, or to the holders of various types of licenses. If there was treasure on the land, it didn't belong to the Army. In fact, a good case could be made that it belonged to the Noss family.

Ova Noss contacted the two senators from New Mexico to enlist their aid. In December 1952, Senator Dennis Chavez wrote to Brigadier General G.G. Eddy about the White Sands Proving Grounds. Ova Noss also succeeded in convincing Senator Clinton P. Anderson to write Eddy as well. The general, however, ruled that no further operations would be allowed in the Proving Grounds because the paperwork was being prepared to transfer all mineral rights to the government.

The dispute was settled in a federal court that worked out a compromise of sorts. The Army had the right to use the surface of the land and no one would be allowed on the Proving Grounds without the Army's consent.

That didn't settle the matter completely because Ova Noss refused to leave. All she wanted, according to the various letters and documents she sent, was to recover what her late husband had discovered.

It all came to a temporary end in the summer of 1955, when federal marshals escorted her from Victorio Peak. But she wouldn't give up the fight. For the rest of her life, she would engage in activities that would enable her to return to the peak so that she could recover the treasure.

Within months a group led by Gordon Bjornson petitioned the Land Office, suggesting that they had the financial backing to find the treasure. General Eddy agreed to let them on the site for two inspections. Then, however, the group couldn't decide whether to dig out the shaft at the top of the peak found by Doc Noss or search for another entrance rumored to be at the base of the mountain.

Bjornson did write to the Land Office expressing his faith in the story told by Doc and Ova Noss. He even mentioned that Noss had removed eighty-six bars of gold, a statue of pure gold, and relics of Spanish origin.

Bjornson obtained permission from the state to begin his operation. The White Sands command issued a denial of permission. The commanding officer was afraid that allowing Bjornson onto the range would set a precedent that would allow others to petition and make similar claims. That would hinder the Army's mission, which was missile testing.

CAPTAIN LEONARD V. FIEGE FINDS A TREASURE

That didn't prevent other military personnel from exploring portions of White Sands. Victorio Peak, which is only about five or six miles from the western edge of the range, was a popular attraction. In 1958, four men, two on active duty with the Air

Force at Holloman Air Force Base, found what they believed was an entrance into the caverns that Noss located more than twenty years earlier.

Captain Leonard V. Fiege, in an affidavit signed later, claimed that he had entered the cavern. It was dark and dusty and hard to breathe. Fiege said he sat down on a pile of rocks to catch his breath and relax. He noticed then that the rocks were not rocks, but, according to him, smelted gold bars about the size of house bricks.

In his flashlight beam, he saw other stacks of similar bricks. Some of them were visible out in the open while others were lost in the dimness of the cave and the dust hanging in the air.

Fiege returned to the opening to find his friends. He was sick and dirty, but once he had told them what he had found, they were interested in returning to the gold. Two of the men were too large to slip through the opening into the main part of the cave, but Fiege and Tom Berlett continued on until they came to the stacks of gold.

While in the cave, Fiege and Berlett talked about what they should do. Neither was familiar with the laws governing the discovery of treasure on a military reservation, nor were they aware that the White Sands command did not hold the mineral rights to anything found on the range. In any case, neither Fiege nor Berlett carried any of the gold from the cave. Or, at least, Fiege later claimed that they had not removed anything.

Fiege said that they did their best to seal off the passage that led to the gold chamber. Fiege told several people that he had caved in the roof and walls to make it look as if the tunnel came to a dead end.

Unlike some of the others, Fiege did show a certain intelligence. He went to the Judge Advocate's (JAG) Office at Holloman Air Force Base and conferred with Colonel Sigmund I. Gasiewicz.

Gasiewicz called the Land Office in Santa Fe and spoke to Oscar Jordan, a Land Office attorney. Gasiewicz said that an officer assigned to the command at Holloman had found a gold bar on White Sands, a different command structure. Holloman is an air force base and White Sands is an army post.

Jordan suggested that the gold be sent to the Department of the Treasury or to the Secret Service office in Albuquerque. It was Jordan's assumption that Fiege had brought a bar of gold to the JAG office. Both Fiege and Gasiewicz would deny that this had happened.

They decided to form a corporation to protect what Fiege had found. They would contact the various governmental agencies to make sure they violated no laws, and to make a formal application to enter White Sands for a search and retrieval of the gold.

It took them three years to work their way through the maze. In May 1961, Fiege and his group began to seriously petition for permission to enter the missile range to search for the treasure. Fiege met with Major General John Shinkle, then the commander of the missile range. Fiege explained that they merely wanted the opportunity to recover a few bars of gold. Shinkle denied the request.

That wasn't the end of it, however. Fiege and his group visited the director of the Mint to ask for permission to recover the gold. The director wrote to the Secretary of the Army asking that permission be granted, not because he believed there was gold to be found or any treasure hidden on the range, but because the Mint had been bothered by so many requests for additional information. The Secret Service said that there was a real possibility that nongold bars had been placed in the cave by Noss in some kind of con game.

IS IT ALL A HOAX?

Jim Eckles, writing in the White Sands Missile Range post news-paper, reported an interesting confirmation to that one point. An old-timer in El Paso told him that Noss would buy copper bars in Orogrande, New Mexico and take them to El Paso to have them gold plated.

Other stories tend to corroborate this. Noss, as he tried to sell the gold, often arrived at the meetings with gold-painted bricks. He said it was because he didn't trust those who were buying the gold, always wanting to see the money before he produced the real gold. In all his dealings with various individuals, he never produced a solid-gold brick, though he did show people small amounts of gold and gold bars that could have been gold plated.

Even with all the confusion, the Mint was interested in solv-ing the mystery once and for all. The Secretary of the Army asked Shinkle for his opinion. The general responded that he would deny entry to the base unless he received permission from the Army to allow a search. He didn't want to set a precedent that would haunt them in the future.

On August 5, 1961, Fiege and his group were allowed to enter the range and work at Victorio Peak. For five days Fiege and his partners tried to enter the tunnel that he had sealed in 1958, but failed to do so. General Shinkle eventually had enough of it and told them to cease their operations.

More requests were made by Fiege. One of the points in his favor was the report that he and Berlett had been given lie detec-tor tests. Both men are reported to have passed them. It gave added importance to their stories.

On September 20, General Shinkle notified the Secret Service he would allow Fiege back on missile range. He would be restricted to the tunnel he'd found and not allowed to begin any new excavations.

Work continued periodically for the next five weeks under the surveillance of Captain Swanner, an officer stationed at the missile range. In late October, according to the records at the missile range, two men were caught trespassing. Swanner ordered them from the area, but not before they had demanded a piece of the action.

The men told Ova Noss that the Army was working on Victorio Peak. Noss accused the Army of trying to steal her treasure and, in December 1961, Shinkle shut down the operation and excluded all from the range who were not engaged in missile research activities.

It should be noted that Jim Eckles, in his reports on the story, makes the fine distinction between what has been reported and the actual facts. The Army was not engaged in the retrieval operation. They allowed a group onto the range who had made a claim. Given the laws of the land, Fiege's claim was as real as that of Ova Noss.

OVA NOSS AND THE CONTINUED SEARCH

The next assault on Victorio Peak came in 1962, when the Gaddis Mining Company, working with the Museum of New Mexico in Santa Fe, began operations. Since it seemed to be a state sponsored research trip, one designed to uncover artifacts of archaeological significance, the Army was inclined to permit access to the range. On June 20, 1963, a license was granted to the Gaddis Mining Company for a thirty day exploration.

Using a variety of techniques, the team tried to map the interior of the peak, searching for large void areas that would indicate caverns. They also built roads to lead to the various important sites, including one to the top of the peak.

They were unable to accomplish all this in the original thirty days and an extension was granted. They dug a number of small test holes ranging in depth from 18 to 175 feet. They also dug their own tunnel into the side of the peak, trying to gain access to the caverns, but failed.

The Gaddis Mining Company is reported to have spent a quarter of a million dollars in their attempt to find treasure. Another seven thousand was requested by the missile range for reimbursement for monies spent in the support of those activities.

As with the Fiege expedition, nothing was found that would suggest that any gold was hidden and nothing of any interest was located in the sixty days of the Gaddis Mining Company operation.

It was during this same period that the Department of the Army asked Ova Noss to sign a consent document allowing the Army to search. What it said was that she waived all rights to sue the Army or the government "for alleged unlawful taking and withholding of her personal property."

Ova Noss's attorney, Phil Koury, thought this a bad idea on her part, but she had already signed the document when he learned of it. Koury asked, "Why would the Army insist on such a waiver? It was an indirect admission that there had been unauthorized intrusion into the Noss Cavern by military personnel; so it was deemed necessary to eliminate Ova's right to resort to litigation to recapture the gold bars."

There is an alternative explanation that makes as much sense. No actual proof had ever been presented that gold was stored inside Victorio Peak. Only Doc Noss had ever claimed to see real treasure there. Only Doc Noss had ever brought out any of the gold. Fiege said he had seen stacks of gold bars, but they had been covered in dust, and he admitted he was feeling sick at the time.

It would seem that the Army was attempting to guard against the real possibility that once the cavern was opened, nothing would be found in it. Then Ova Noss would believe that the Army or the government had beaten her into the cave and "stolen" the treasure that belonged to her. It would make no difference if the gold had been there or not. It would make no difference if the story was a myth or not. Ova Noss would file suit and the Army would be defenseless to protect itself from those claims.

Ova Noss, however, was making money on the story of the treasure. Various investment groups, convinced of the validity of the story, would approach her, buy a portion of her rights to the treasure, and then begin their attempts to force the military to allow them onto Victorio Peak.

In 1973, for example, a syndicate from Salt Lake City offered $150,000 for an interest in her rights to the treasure. They would pay $25,000 immediately and $5,000 a month. They wanted 51 percent of Ova Noss's interest but were negotiated to 49 percent.

This time there was a hint of real treasure. One of the men, identified as John Walton, according to Koury, said that he had seen twenty-two gold bars that he had been told came from the Noss treasure. He had counted the bars himself and it was estimated they were worth about $6 million.

Ova Noss received the $25,000 but there were never any monthly payments. Koury eventually notified Walton's attorney that the failure to make the required payments nullified the contract. The attorney could shed no light on why the payments had not been made.

OTHER CLAIMS
TO THE TREASURE

Others entered into the arena. F. Lee Bailey contacted officials in Washington, D.C. asking for help because his clients had come into possession of a number of gold bars. Bailey made it clear that forty of his clients lived in the White Sands area and knew the exact location of the gold.

Bailey was skeptical but was provided with one of the bars for analysis. Bailey sent it to the Treasury for testing. It was 60 percent gold and 40 percent copper. The problem is that fourteen-karat gold is about 58 percent gold and 42 percent copper. It was noted that old gold ingots were often far from pure. No real conclusion could be drawn from the tests.

Bailey would eventually say that there were two groups involved: a small group who found the treasure and a larger group made of businessmen who were financing various operations including the legal maneuvering.

It was also in 1973 that several people sneaked onto the missile range to dynamite a rock wall in a side canyon of Victorio Peak. It was claimed that if you knew how to read the pictographs found on the rock wall, you could find the treasure. They wanted to remove that information.

Bailey and his group continued to make claims. The original story they told, of 292 bars of gold, escalated into thousands of gold bars. At one point someone claimed that more than two hundred billion dollars was hidden in Victorio Peak. The more rational pointed out that Fort Knox held just over six billion dollars in gold.

Others came forward, including Roscoe Parr, who claimed that Noss had told him how to find the gold and how to divide it once it was claimed. There was nothing in writing from Noss, but Noss had asked Parr to make sure his wishes were carried out after his death.

Other groups were formed around Fiege; the second Mrs. Noss, Violet Noss Yancy; something called the Shriver group; Expeditions Unlimited, a Florida based treasure hunting group; and, of course, Ova Noss.

Ova Noss tried to end it all by suing the Army for a billion dollars. In the documents filed with the court, she claimed that it would take no more than forty-eight hours to find the gold with no more than four people making the search. Once they had located the treasure, they would place the gold with the appropriate governmental agencies for safekeeping until the ownership could be determined. The suit was dismissed.

A compromise among all the claimants was arranged by Norm Scott who used his Expeditions Unlimited to represent them all. The Army saw the wisdom of this and agreed to it. Operation Goldfinder was postponed twice, but in March 1977 the search finally began.

And failed.

Just as the searches that had preceded it, Operation Goldfinder failed to produce any evidence that any gold was hidden on Victorio Peak. One group of claimants tried to "salt" the site with fake gold bars, but were caught and ordered out by Scott.

What was most valuable, from the Army's point of view, was that those claiming something was hidden in Victorio Peak had had their chance to search. They found nothing. The Army then shut down all operations, claimed that nothing was hidden, and that no additional searches would be allowed in the foreseeable future.

Scott held a final press conference after the failure to find any gold, or any evidence that any gold had ever been hidden there.

Scott did not consider the search a failure. He pointed out to the press that the objectives had been realized, with one exception.

That exception surrounds the claims of Doc Noss. Those accepting the Noss story point out that it wasn't proven that gold wasn't there. This is arguing in circles because it was proven that "no treasure was found in the various locations where most of the claimants told us a gold cache is hidden." They are now claiming that the gold was in those areas not searched.

Even with the negative results, without any physical evidence that the gold had ever been there, with only the testimony of a man who was a con man and a charlatan, there are those who still believed that a huge treasure was hidden in Victorio Peak.

Operation Goldfinder cost $87,000. Scott said that he had no plans for another search. Such a project would cost half a million dollars and would take a couple of months. At the conclusion of the press conference, the commander of the White Sands Missile Range closed the range to any further search for treasure.

That wasn't the end of it. Ova Noss believed there was gold and that it belonged to her. For decades others had believed as well, providing her with encouragement and money. She was not going to let her dream die.

In 1979 Ova Noss returned to Victorio Peak and posed for photographs. At that time, according to a story by Jim Eckles in the *Missile Ranger*, she said, "Like they say. There's gold in them thar hills." She died later that same year without ever finding her treasure.

The search didn't die with her. Her grandson, Terry Delonas, had accompanied Ova Noss to Victorio Peak. It was clear that he was going to continue the family tradition. He formed the Ova Noss Family Partnership.

SOME ARCHAEOLOGICAL EVIDENCE

One of the main problems has always been a lack of any kind of evidence for a treasure in the region. If the Partnership, or anyone else, had been able to demonstrate that something was hidden, the Army would have been more receptive to additional searches of range property.

Some archaeological evidence was discovered in 1988 in the pictographs and petroglyphs that dotted the rocks around Victorio Peak. For the most part, these had been ignored, the assumption being that the markings were drawn by the Indians who lived in the region. The January 28, 1993 issue of *The Courier*, published in Hatch, reported on "The Mystery People."

Gene Ballinger wrote that the markings were a type of writing known as Ogam and that the writers were of Celtic origin. Ballinger claimed that the oral tradition of the Indians spoke of a group of "white" Indians. These white Indians lived in southern New Mexico about the time of Christ and died out some thousand years later.

Ogam, according to one expert, Dr. Arnold Murray, Pastor of the Shepherds Chapel and director of the Shepherds Chapel Network, is an ancient form of writing which, until recently, couldn't be read. According to a March 4, 1993 edition of *The Courier*, Dr. Barry Fell first discovered and isolated the Ogam alphabet while teaching at Harvard. The samples in southern New Mexico, according to these experts, dated from 2500 B.C. to 250 B.C.

It is the belief of various experts that the caves of Victorio Peak were used as warehouses. Gold mined for the last two thousand years was stored there because there wasn't a means of moving the bulk of the treasure from New Mexico. When the Celts died out, the Indians, including the Navajo, Apache, and Pueblo Indians, fought over and then stored more treasure in the caves.

According to one of Ballinger's articles, the last treasure was placed in the caves in 1886. Apache warriors raiding the stage lines had stolen strong boxes from Wells Fargo. That would explain the boxes seen by Doc Noss about fifty years later. And it would explain the amount of treasure in the cave. Various groups had been adding to it for over two thousand years.

Ballinger, listening to Murray and Fell, is of the opinion that the finds of Ogam around Victorio Peak are of immense archaeological significance. The Spanish sword and other artifacts found and held by the Ova Noss Family Partnership establish the validity of the original claims. If that is brought forward, then the Army would be required to open the range for further exploration.

ANOTHER ASSAULT ON VICTORIO PEAK

In early 1989, the partnership again approached the Department of the Army seeking permission to begin negotiations to return to Victorio Peak. Assistance from Norm Scott and his Expeditions Unlimited from Florida was again enlisted.

This time, before any work was done, the vast body of government regulations were brought to bear. Before anyone was allowed back on the range and the peak, environmental impact statements, archaeological research statements, and various other documents were to be prepared. Once those reports were submitted and approved, then the work could begin.

It became clear from the reports that the 1962 Gaddis Mining Company expedition to Victorio Peak had been sponsored, at least in part, by the Noss family. They had been given their fourty-eight hours and four men nearly thirty years earlier and had found nothing. That didn't stop them from making claims that the government was preventing them from finding and recovering their treasure.

The environmental impact statements and the archaeological assessments were completed and submitted, reviewed and approved. Then a rider to the 1990 Appropriations Bill provided the last push. It said, "The Secretary of the Army may, subject to such terms and conditions as the Secretary considers appropriate to protect the interests of the United States, issue a revocable license to the Ova Noss Family Partnership."

The rider also made it clear that the Partnership would reimburse the Department of the Army for expenses. The rider provided a mechanism so that the reimbursement was directed to the missile range rather than the Department of the Army. In Fiscal Year 1990, the range collected $122,000 from the Partnership for range support.

The Partnership has been allowed on the range for a new search. As late as April 1995, they had found nothing to indicate that any treasure had ever been held in the caves of Victorio Peak. They recovered an old board from a tunnel that they believed had been left by Doc Noss many years ago.

VICTORIO PEAK: WHAT IS THE TRUTH?

There is no good historical evidence to suggest that any gold was ever hidden in Victorio Peak by anyone other than Doc Noss. He did, at times, attempt to sell gold to various people, but those attempts always ended with Noss trying to peddle gold-plated bricks. No sizable treasure was ever brought out, and no one has been able to verify its existence.

There is one point that must be made. In the 1930s, a law was passed making it illegal for private citizens to own gold bullion. There were exceptions made for jewelry and coins. Noss, however, mentioned seeing precious stones and gems in the cave as well as gold. These could be exchanged legally for cash and would have financed any recovery operations necessary. He could have retained the services of any attorney he wanted to protect his claim. Noss had no need for any outside investors.

The single piece of documentation—the receipt from the Mint—vanished. Noss allegedly had it in his possession, but it disappeared after his death. The Mint had no record that Noss had ever visited them.

Given the actions of Noss, it seems unlikely that he ever found anything. The evidence, studied under the harsh, cold light of objectivity, suggests there was never any treasure.

There is one final point to be made. It is clear from the record that the Army and the officials at White Sands Missile Range have treated everyone involved in this affair with honor and respect. When Victorio Peak is finally ripped open and the caves exposed, there will be no treasure because there never was one.

8

INCA GOLD?

ALABAMA

THIS STORY, HANDED DOWN from generation to generation, concerns the documented loss of gold found in Peru and legends of treasure in Red Bone Cave. Indians guarded it for decades, sharing the secret with only one white man who failed in his attempt to recover the loot.

According to the legend, Hernando de Soto, who explored parts of the southern United States in 1540, carried the treasure with him. He landed in what is now Tampa Bay in 1538, marched northward and then turned west, heading eventually into Arkansas. Finally he turned again, this time entering into what is now Mississippi and Alabama. In October 1540, he reached the Tennessee River area where he halted to build his winter camp.

De Soto and his men had no trouble at first with the local Chickasaw. In fact, the chief came to the Spanish camp with gifts of corn and grain that he claimed earlier white travelers had taught them to cultivate. In return, de Soto ordered his men to butcher a couple of the pigs they had brought with them. The Indians seemed to enjoy the pork.

   In fact, the Indians enjoyed the pork so much that many of
the Spanish pigs began to disappear. De Soto and his men caught
four Chickasaws who had tried to steal a couple of the pigs one
night. Three of the Indians were executed by the Spanish and a
fourth was sent back to the village. As a warning to the others,
de Soto ordered that both of his hands be cut off at the wrist.

   The Chickasaw chief didn't react to the death and mutila-
tion of his braves. Maybe he thought they deserved what they got
for stealing, or maybe he thought they deserved it for getting
caught. At any rate, there was no hostile response by the Indians.

   Emboldened by that, de Soto then demanded that the chief
surrender two hundred Indian women for servants. That was too
much for the chief. Instead of sending the women, the Chickasaws
attacked the Spanish camp. De Soto and a few survivors were
forced to flee, leaving most of their equipment, wagons, and other
possessions behind.

If de Soto had plans to return to that location to recover the treasure and other equipment, he never made it. A few months later he died near the Mississippi River close to present day Memphis, Tennessee, and was buried on a bluff overlooking the river.

The Chickasaws had no use for the heavy yellow metal the Spanish had left behind them. Oh, they knew what it was and how important it was to white men. They had seen explorers searching for it and knew the trouble it caused everyone who came into contact with it. They didn't want more white men to follow the last. They gathered the gold and hid it in one of the many caves along the Tennessee River.

Rumors, stories, and legends about the treasure swirled, but no one else came to search for the gold. Maybe those who heard the story discounted it. After all, it makes little sense for de Soto to have dragged wagons of gold with him, especially all the way from Peru. If he had the loot, why not leave it with his ships? Or why not bury it near Tampa Bay?

However, the story didn't end there. One hundred fifty years later, at the beginning of the nineteenth century, a white man entered the land of the Chickasaw. He wanted to trap and hunt on the tribal lands, which were filled with game. Permission was granted by the chief.

The trapper thought nothing about that. There was more than enough for everyone, and there had been little conflict between the whites and the Indians. The legend, however, gives another reason for that permission.

Royal lineage passes through the mother. The chief had a daughter, but he needed a grandson to take over when he was too old to rule. His daughter hadn't found a man who appealed to her. Until the trapper appeared.

Several weeks after the trapper arrived, while sleeping in a shelter provided by the Chickasaw, he was kidnapped. His hands were bound and he was blindfolded. His captors told him that he had nothing to fear because they meant him no harm at the moment.

He was led from the village into the surrounding forest. Throughout the night and into the following day, they took him farther from the village. They rested from time to time, but always pushed on. They ate little and drank periodically, but never stopped for long.

When his blindfold slipped during the day, he recognized the area. The water and the white cliffs were a long way from the Chickasaw village, but he had hunted and fished the area. While he waited, his captors put a canoe into the river so they could cross it.

Having crossed the river, the Indians checked the ropes and blindfold. They then climbed a steep hill and finally stopped. There was a sudden coolness and the footing changed. The trapper realized they were in a cave.

They then stopped for what seemed to be a long time. Finally they began walking again, this time at a much slower pace because the slope was quite a bit steeper. They stopped once again. The blindfold was removed and he was allowed the first opportunity to look at his surroundings.

Standing with him was the village chief. Behind him, visible in the flickering light of the torches, were stacks of gold and silver bars. There were wooden chests, rotting away and spilling the treasure within them. There were jewels, both emeralds and rubies. Around the treasure were the skeletons of several men. These were the Indians who had originally helped hide the treasure who had been sacrificed as ghostly or spiritual guards.

He was allowed to walk forward where the gold bars were stacked from the floor to the ceiling. He was allowed to examine the chests of treasure, slipping a medallion with a large red stone into his pocket. He was allowed to handle the gold coins that had spilled to the cave's floor.

All of it, he was told, was his. He could keep all the treasure. There was a single condition. He had to marry the chief's daughter. And once that happened, he would become the village chief. Once the marriage took place, the treasure was his.

The trapper stood there, stunned. Here was almost unimaginable wealth. There were literally tons of gold. More than he could spend in a lifetime. More than he could spend in a dozen lifetimes. But the catch was too much. He knew that marrying the chief's daughter would mean that he could never leave the area. He would be watched day and night and if he did escape, he couldn't get away, especially if he tried to carry anything out with him. What good was tons of gold if he could never get to a place where it would be worth something?

The chief told him that he would not be harmed, no matter what his decision. Sure that he could later find the cave, he decided to refuse the deal. However, he didn't tell the chief that immediately. Instead he said that he wanted to think about it for a time. He had a wife and child waiting for him at one of the forts in the area.

The trapper was then blindfolded again and they started out of the cave. After several hours, they were back in the forest, far from the cave. As soon as the opportunity came, he killed both his captors and dumped the bodies into the river. He then returned to the village, confident in the knowledge that no one there knew what had happened. He had been taken out of the village secretly, no one had seen him leave, so no one knew he had been with the chief.

After several weeks, when he had finished his trapping, he left the village. He had wanted to wait long enough so that the Chickasaws wouldn't be suspicious of him.

Once safely back at a French fort at White Apple Village, he told his story to another man. To prove the truth, he showed the man the jeweled medallion he had taken. It didn't take much for the trapper to convince the man that a fortune waited for the men clever enough to find it.

They searched for weeks, but only at night, hiding during the day. They crawled into dozens of caves but couldn't find the right one. After months, the trapper's friend abandoned the search to return to civilization.

Now the trapper needed a new plan. He returned to the Chickasaw village. The old chief, now missing for over a year, had left no successor, so a new chief was "elected." The daughter had left the main village and was now living in a smaller one. He married her so that he could continue his search. Now he was a member of the tribe and, because his wife was no longer the daughter of the chief, he was free to roam.

For years he searched for the treasure, trying to figure out why he couldn't find it. There weren't that many caves along the section of the river he had seen. He thought about it endlessly, and then, one night, in a fit of inspiration, believed he had figured it out. Just before they had entered the chamber with the treasure, and just after they left it, they had paused for a very long time. The Chickasaws were concealing the tunnel where the treasure was hidden.

With this new knowledge, he returned to the caves, searching the walls of dozens of caverns. Even with that, he couldn't locate the treasure. He was doing something wrong, but couldn't understand what it was.

Eventually he gave up. His Chickasaw wife had died and he returned to his own people. He traveled the region, inducing others to buy him drinks or meals for his tale of the lost gold that had been taken from the Spanish.

Like so many of these stories, there are problems with it. Indians took the precious gold from the Spanish. They couldn't use it, but hid it from the white man. There is no corroboration for this, though it is well documented that de Soto did travel the area in search of treasure. He may have found some. The Cherokee did mine and work gold in a limited fashion and de Soto might have found some of that. There is almost no possibility, however, that de Soto would have been transporting a large treasure taken from the Incas in Central America.

Historically speaking, however, we can document that the Spanish crown, which was supposed to share in all treasure found, never received everything it was entitled to. De Soto left much of the treasure in Central America simply because he didn't have the ships to carry it all back to Spain. Much of that has never been located.

So, could there be a large treasure from Central America hidden in an Alabama cave? It's possible, but not very likely. But that small chance is enough to fire gold fever in treasure hunters. Maybe one of them will get lucky. After all, there is as much chance of finding this horde of Inca gold as there is of winning a state lottery. For some, that is more than enough incentive.

9

THE BEALE CODES

—

VIRGINIA

EVERYONE BELIEVES THAT THE Lost Dutchman Mine is hidden somewhere in the Superstition Mountains. In the Oak Island search, the exact location is known. With the Beale Treasure, there is a code that, if cracked, could provide the location of more than ten million dollars. The Beale Codes provide some documentation about the existence of the treasure.

The story begins with Robert Morriss, a hotel man in Lynchburg, Virginia in 1862. He called on a close friend, James Ward, and asked to meet him in one of the hotel offices later. When they were comfortable, Morriss began to tell Ward his tale of treasure.

In 1820, Morriss was manager of the Washington Hotel. In Janaury of that year he first met Thomas Jefferson Beale. Beale arrived at the hotel with two other men, who left him there for the rest of the winter while they went on to Richmond.

Morriss told Ward that Beale left at the end of February 1821 and came back about two years later. As before, he stayed for two months and then left. However, before he left, according to

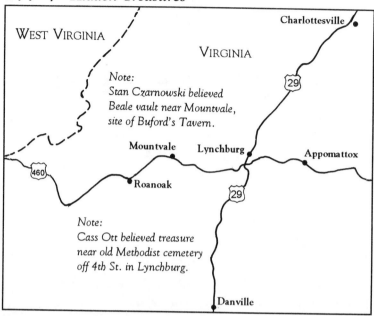

Morriss, he asked Morriss to guard a small box that contained important papers. Morriss had no idea what was in the box, other than some documents he was to protect. In May 1822, Morriss received a letter from Beale that provided a few clues.

It reinforced the original instructions and the importance of the papers. Beale wrote that if he, or someone authorized by him, had not asked for the box, Morriss was to open it. Those papers would mean nothing unless the key was provided and the key was in the hands of another man in St. Louis. The key would be mailed in June 1832. Until he received the key, Morriss would not be able to decipher the papers.

That was the last Morriss ever heard from Beale. No authorized person arrived and no letter came in June 1832. Morriss then showed remarkable restraint. He did not open the box in 1832, but waited, according to the story, until 1845 before he had the locks broken.

Morriss found two letters addressed to him and some papers covered with numbers. Those papers would later become known as the Beale Code.

One of the letters was of no importance to understanding the story or the codes, at least according to Morriss. The other was a long letter that told all of Beale's story. The real story began, not in 1862, when Morriss invited his friend to the hotel, but in April 1817.

In that month and year Beale, with a number of companions, left Virginia to explore the west. They reached St. Louis in May and then pressed on, arriving in Santa Fe, New Mexico about the first of December.

In the spring some of the men decided to explore the territory around Santa Fe. They didn't return when expected, and Beale and his friends decided to send out a rescue party. It proved to be unnecessary; two of the men arrived in Santa Fe with tales of gold and silver.

The hunting party had worked their way north, chasing an abundance of game until they were 250 miles north of Santa Fe, in southern Colorado. They had stopped to camp, and were gathering wood when one of the men found gold.

When Beale arrived on the scene, not only were his friends digging gold, but also they had made a silver strike. They kept digging the ore out of the ground, refining it as best they could with the crude methods available to them, and then decided to return some of the treasure to Virginia. They all knew of a cave near Buford's Tavern in Bedford County where they planned to hide the gold and silver.

Unfortunately, when they got there, they learned the cave was too well known. Local farmers were using it to store their produce. A new site, less well known, had to be found. Once they had found a suitable site, the treasure was buried. Beale, and the men with him, then headed to Lynchburg, Virginia, to search for a trustworthy man to hold the codes. Those were entrusted to Morriss.

Beale said that he then returned to the mines to help out. He made another trip with treasure to Virginia, adding to the wealth that was hidden. It was during the second trip that Morriss was given the box containing the codes and instructions.

The letter told Morriss that the codes told exactly where the treasure was hidden (Code No. 1), the contents of the vault or repository (Code No. 2), and finally a listing of the men involved and their families (Code No. 3). Beale was told that if no one showed up to collect the box, he was to open it, and upon receipt of the key, recover the treasure and split it into thirty-one equal shares. One share was his payment for carrying out instructions. The rest was to be given to those whose family members had participated in the mining of the gold and silver.

At the time he shared the information with Ward, Morriss was eighty-four years old. He wanted someone he trusted to take over the task. Morriss had never been able to decipher any of the codes; he had never received the key. Morriss wanted Ward to try to decipher the codes.

Ward took over the task, trying everything that he could think of. In 1885, he wrote a pamphlet called *The Beale Papers*. In the pamphlet he explained the whole story. Unfortunately, before he could begin sale of the pamphlet, a fire swept through the print shop, destroying most copies.

The surviving copies have been studied for years by treasure hunters, cryptologists, and interested parties. In his pamphlet, Ward told of his attempts to figure out the code. He spent years at it, causing his family grief as all other thoughts were pushed from his mind. The Beale codes became a personal obsession.

His perseverance was rewarded. He broke the code on the second piece of paper. For those interested, Ward detailed how he had done it. He numbered every word in the *Declaration of Independence*. He then substituted the words in the *Declaration* for the numbers in the code. That wasn't quite right, but when he used the first letter of each numbered word to spell out the words, he had the code.

In other words, the first numbers in Beale's Code No. 2 were 115, 73, 24, 818, and so on. The 115th word is "instituted." The first letter of the second code is "I." The 73rd word is "hold." The second letter of the code is "H." By going through the entire code in that fashion, Ward was able to read the message, which was:

> I have deposited in the county of Bedford about four miles from Buford's in an excavation or vault six feet below the surface of the ground the following articles belonging jointly to the parties whose names are given in Number Three herewith. The first deposit consisted of ten hundred and fourteen pounds of gold and thirty-eight and twelve pounds of silver deposited November 1819. The second was made December 1821 and consisted of nineteen hundred and seven pounds of gold and twelve hundred and eighty-eight of silver. Also jewels obtained in St. Louis in exchange to save transportation and valued at thirteen thousand dollars. The above is securely packed in iron pots with iron covers. The vault is roughly lined with stones and the vessels rest on solid stone and are covered with others. Paper Number One describes the exact locality of the vault so that no difficulty will be had in finding it.

Ward, of course, thought that he would now be able to easily crack the other codes. He understood how they had been fashioned. He tried using the *Declaration of Independence* on the other papers, but it was not the key. Still, he knew more than Morriss had when he told him the story.

The mission given to Morriss and passed to Ward was inherited, after a fashion, by N.H. Hazelwood. One of Ward's pamphlets found its way to Hazelwood. He then asked Clayton I. Hart to copy the code. Hart asked what the numbers meant and was told it was a code to find a treasure buried about eighty years earlier.

With Hazelwood's permission, Hart kept a copy of the three codes and then spent all his time trying to break them. With his brother, George L. Hart, Sr., they numbered hundreds of works that Beale might have had. They tried various methods such as skipping the first word, numbering the works backward, skipping words, but they couldn't find the key to the other two codes.

They even delved into the ridiculous. Clayton became interested in hypnosis and tried to use it. Hypnotizing a young man who was a good subject, he asked him where the treasure was hidden. Not surprisingly, the young man told them exactly where it was. But, of course, they didn't find it.

When the young man was hypnotized again, he declared that he could see the treasure. They needed to dig two feet to the right. Clayton later came back to try again, but he still found nothing.

In 1924, the brothers learned about Colonel George Fabyan, who was an expert in breaking codes. George Hart sent the codes to Fabyan, who responded in 1925 that such a code could not be broken without a key.

Al Masters, reporting in *Saga's Special 1976 Treasure*, wrote that Cass Ott, a refrigeration engineer in Chicago, read about the codes and spent time studying them. Although his son, among others, told him to give it up, Ott continued anyway, and after a short time said he had broken the first code.

With this decoded letter in hand, Ott, with his son, headed to Lynchburg. He found the landmarks based on his decoded version of the first letter. Included in this was the old Methodist Cemetery off Fourth Street. He also found the faded pyramid of brands on a tree that were Beale's treasure marks.

The problem for Ott was that the location of the treasure vault was on city property. He needed permission, which he eventually got, providing he would split the treasure with the city. Ott had nothing to lose and agreed.

In May 1970, all was set. City workers and equipment were employed. They located what they thought was the proper site, and began to dig. Other than metallic junk, they found nothing. They dug down to a rock ledge that prevented them from digging farther.

Another man, Stan Czarnowski, also claimed to have decoded the message. He believed the vault was near Montvale (the site of Buford's Tavern, on Route 460 East). He found an old ice house that was six feet underground. Below that he found an excavation he claimed was roughly lined with stones as Beale had claimed. The vault found by Czarnowski was empty.

It was Czarnowski's belief that he had found the Beale vault, but that someone, possibly Beale himself, had returned. Whoever it was, he had emptied the vault fifty or sixty years earlier. There had once been treasure there.

Both Ott and Czarnowski claimed to have decoded the paper that held specific directions to the vault. Both dug for the treasure and both failed to find it. But the two men had dug at two widely separated locations. That could easily mean that neither had adequately deciphered the code or that the directions weren't as specific as others had thought.

Not long after Czarnowski's failure to recover the treasure, A.B. Chandler of Richmond, Virginia announced that he, too, had broken the code. The whole story, according to his work, was a hoax. There was no treasure, just the ridiculous documents that had hundreds tearing up Virginia real estate in a futile quest for wealth.

That conclusion was disputed by those who had searched for the Beale treasure for decades. One man, Hiram Herbert, said that he didn't believe Chandler's report. According to Herbert, too many people with too many computers had tried to decode the letters. He believed the story to be genuine. Of course it could be said the code is genuine, but that doesn't mean that the treasure ever existed.

As late as the early 1990s people were still searching for the Beale treasure. *Unsolved Mysteries* was even present for the search by a couple of treasure hunters. When the digging was finished, the treasure still hadn't been found. They, of course, said they would continue to search.

There are so many stories of treasures found and then lost. Few contain any sort of documentation. Most are little more than rumors of wealth that have, over the years, come to gain the status of established fact. Some are based on nothing other than speculation. The Beale treasure is one of the few where there are documents.

There is no doubt that the codes exist. There is no doubt that the codes appeared in the eighteenth century. There is no doubt that they are complex. And there is no doubt that the key to the second code has been found . . . the one that provided little information about the location of the treasure.

The Beale treasure is unique. It is the only one that allows the treasure hunter to remain at home while searching for it. With copies of the codes, and the knowledge of the key to the second, he or she can try to solve the puzzle. If that happens, then a treasure now estimated at between ten and twenty million dollars can be found, payment for a hobby with huge reward for little or no investment other than some time.

10

FORT HUACHUCA

—

ARIZONA

ROBERT JONES, AN ENLISTED man assigned to a communications unit at Fort Huachuca, near Sierra Vista, Arizona, in the summer of 1941, discovered a cache of gold and silver that rivals that claimed at nearby Victorio Peak. And, like Doc Noss, he was unable to carry away any of the treasure that he found, so had no proof that the gold existed.

Jones, with a companion assigned to the same unit, tried to escape the excessive summer heat by driving into the Huachuca Mountains. They stopped in Huachuca Canyon and then began to explore the surrounding territory. Jones noticed an area where the rocky rubble at the base of a cliff was a different color from the surrounding strata. When he walked over to study it, the desert floor collapsed under his weight.

He fell about thirty feet into an underground chamber. Momentarily dazed and only slightly injured, Jones recovered and then called for his friend. In the slanting sunlight pouring through the hole in the roof, Jones saw that he was in a tunnel that disappeared into the solid rock of the canyon wall.

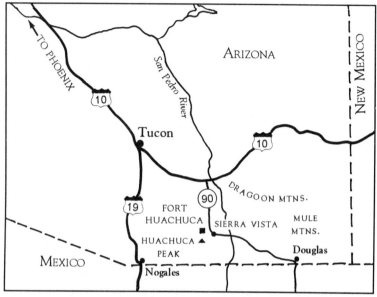

He called for a flashlight, which his friend dropped down to him. The passage slanted downward and Jones followed for quite a long way until he came into a large, carved out chamber lined with stones cemented together as if to brace the walls. It was obvious that it wasn't a natural formation.

More important than the construction of the room was what he found in it. According to Jones, stacked along the wall were metal bars. Jones said there were at least a hundred bars of gold that were about twenty inches long weighing about fifty pounds. Another, similar stack of metal was made of silver bars. A huge chest was filled with gold nuggets and another held gold dust.

On the floor near the chests, Jones found a bottle that held a rolled piece of parchment. Jones pulled it from the bottle, but it was written in Spanish and he couldn't read it. He replaced it, left the bottle, and then walked back to the place into which he had fallen. With the help of his friend, Jones escaped from the tunnel.

Back at the main base, Jones told the story to his company commander who didn't believe it. Neither did the other two officers Jones told. His company first sergeant, Matt Venable, did believe it and tried to interest the commanders in checking the story. They just were uninterested. Tales of lost treasure were common in the southwest. Besides, Jones had brought out nothing to prove his story.

Jones decided his best course of action was to return to the canyon to hide the entrance through which he'd tumbled. Using logs, rocks, and brush, he disguised the hole. He carved two slashes in a nearby tree and his initials into a granite boulder about thirty feet away.

Although both men wanted to return to claim the treasure, the Second World War prevented it. Both were quickly transferred from Arizona. Jones went to the Pacific where he was badly wounded. His friend went to Europe and was killed in the fighting there.

After the war Jones, crippled by his wounds, lived in Dallas with his wife, a nurse. Periodically he returned to Arizona, but his war injuries prevented him from recovering the gold himself. He tried to enlist the assistance of the Army, but military regulations prevented it. Attempts to obtain permission to dig were routinely rejected by military officers.

In 1959, nearly twenty years after he'd fallen into the cave, Jones was interviewed by Major General F.W. Moorman, then post commander at Fort Huachuca. Moorman reviewed Jones's service record and found nothing to convince him that Jones was either a liar or a teller of tall tales. The record revealed that Jones was a good soldier who had served honorably. Moorman required Jones to be evaluated by two Army psychiatrists. Their evaluation revealed nothing other than a belief by the Army doctors that Jones was telling the truth as he knew it.

Given all that, General Moorman granted Jones a license to

dig for two weeks. Jones lined up assistance from a number of parties, promising them a share of the wealth once the treasure was recovered.

Jones had no trouble in returning to the location of the shaft. He found the marks he'd left so many years before and the digging began. It was soon discovered that one wall had collapsed since he had last been there. Tons of rock and debris filled the tunnel and blocked their way. Jones approached the Army and asked permission to bring in some heavy equipment.

The Army went him one better, providing the equipment for him. The bulldozer opened the shaft, digging out the debris to a depth of about ten feet when water began to pour in, stopping them. They were unprepared for the water and it was entering the shaft too fast for them.

Before he could deal with that problem, the time the Army allowed for the excavation had expired. There had been no evidence found that would prove the story of the treasure. Jones was ordered to halt the operation.

But in September 1959, Jones was back, asking permission to resume the search, this time with the proper equipment. The Army quickly granted the necessary permission and Jones returned to his digging.

They used a drill to punch through the top of the chamber, which was right where Jones said it should be. At the same time bulldozers, again provided by the Army, dug out the tunnel. Again the water began to seep into the chambers, but this time Jones had pumps to handle it. He was sure that he would be able to defeat the water.

The water, however, proved to be a formidable enemy. It undermined everything, collapsing the walls of the newly dug tunnels, threatening the workings, and destroying the evidence. Even the men on the equipment were in danger.

A new enemy entered the picture. The news media heard about the search and began to invade the Army post. The Army enacted new regulations and security measures to protect everyone but finally demanded that the operations be shut down. Like the water, the press could not be stopped.

About that same time, a representative from the Treasury Department arrived. He was going to take charge of any treasure found, holding it until ownership could be established. He did mention that the government would get sixty percent with Jones receiving the remaining forty percent if the people who buried it did not claim it. Jones would be required to pay taxes on all treasure he received.

To expedite the digging, a steam shovel was brought in. When more problems were encountered, they decided to dynamite their way into the treasure cavern. But that plan failed, too, filling the passageway with additional tons of debris. There were also indications that the explosion might have collapsed the main cavern.

Again Jones called off the search. He thanked those who had supported and helped him. He did say that he would try to find proper financial backing and return later.

For the rest of his life, Jones tried to interest investors in the treasure. He also tried to gain additional permits and permissions from the military. Colonel Elridge Bacon became the project officer at Fort Huachuca for Jones but he was unable to get the permissions that Jones needed to continue his search.

In 1961, just twenty years after Jones had found the treasure but before he could benefit from it, he died in his sleep. The wounds that he suffered during the war were a contributing factor in shortening his life.

That didn't end the search for the gold. Quest Exploration, a California company, received permission from the Army in 1975 to dig for the treasure. They used the latest technology to explore the canyon with radar and ground sensors. They found no evidence of any caverns. They speculated that any chambers or caverns probably collapsed during the earlier retrieval operations. Quest executives believed the treasure was there. The recovery operation would have to remove tons of rock, dirt, and debris before they would see a dime of gold.

Captain William S. Jameson, who commanded the military police during one of the recovery attempts, had spoken to Jones several times and believed the tale. But more important, Jameson knew that one of the military policemen assigned to security at the Huachuca Canyon site had found a small, hand-dug shaft that contained old Spanish tools, spurs, and coins. It showed that the Spanish had been in the area working some type of mining operation and was one corroboration for the tale of gold.

Like the Victorio Peak controversy, the Army now says that there is no treasure hidden at Fort Huachuca. Opportunities for recovery have been granted and searches have been made, but no gold has ever been recovered. Only one man ever saw it, and he waited a long time for a chance to get back into the tunnel. He has been dead for more than thirty years.

The differences in the two cases should be pointed out as well. Doc Noss was an obvious con man, and he worked very hard to sell faked gold bricks to anyone foolish enough to buy them. Jones never did that. The tunnels were there, where he said they were and the digging operations did uncover them. It seems that nature stepped in to prevent him, or anyone, from finding the treasure.

Since 1975, there has been no real effort to recover the gold. The Army routinely refuses permission to dig in Huachuca Canyon. They say they don't believe in the myth of the treasure. But several years ago an old desert rat said that he had seen the Army was working in the area with a couple of bulldozers. Maybe that was coincidence. Maybe.

PIRATE CACHES,
GANGSTER GOLD,
AND
STOLEN MONEY

11

JEAN LAFITTE'S TREASURE CACHES

—

LOUISIANA

THERE IS NO DOUBT THAT JEAN Lafitte was a pirate who raided the Caribbean at the beginning of the nineteenth century. There is no doubt that he assisted Andrew Jackson in winning the Battle of New Orleans in 1814. And there is no doubt that Lafitte buried treasure along the Gulf Coast from Pensacola, Florida to Corpus Christi, Texas. A few smaller caches have been found, establishing the reality of those treasure troves.

Lafitte was born in France, sometime around 1780. Or maybe he was born in Spain. Records from that time are sparse and frequently inaccurate or missing.

Little is known about his life before his appearance in New Orleans, but some facts have been found. He apparently served aboard a French privateer, but eventually emigrated to the West

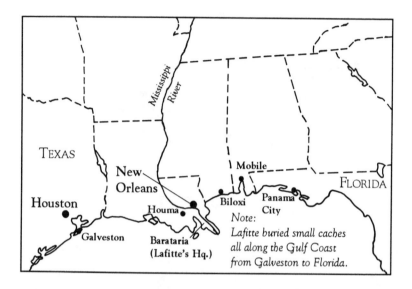

TEXAS

New
Orleans

Houston

Galveston

Houma

Bataria
(Lafitte's Hq.)

Biloxi

Mobile

Panama
City

FLORIDA

Note:

*Lafitte buried small caches
all along the Gulf Coast
from Galveston to Florida.*

Indies to make his fortune. He became a merchant in a number of legal endeavors and was soon joined by his older brother, Pierre. He was married for a time, to Marie de Montagnac.

The story is that Lafitte, his wife, and his brother then decided to return to France aboard the *Piquant*. They were intercepted by a Spanish ship and boarded. The Spanish captain executed the sailors and then abandoned the passengers on one of the many little islands in the area. Before they were rescued, Lafitte's wife became ill. Although rescued quickly, she died several days later.

Lafitte had lost everything, including his wife, in the raid by the Spanish. There was nothing left for him. With his brother, he began his own career as a privateer . . . a pirate. Rumors suggested that he was ruthless with the Spanish, but he was more often merciful when the victims were American, English, or French. Not always, but sometimes.

Lafitte made war on the Spanish. He killed all he captured, even when they surrendered. He burned the ships he didn't want, destroyed the cargo he couldn't use, and then sailed off looking for his next victims. They didn't have to be Spanish, but he claimed he only attacked the Spanish. Frequently he made mistakes.

Interestingly, Lafitte was not without some sort of official backing for his exploits. The Republic of Cartagena, a city in Colombia, granted Lafitte a privateer's commission. With this semilegal commission, he was authorized to attack, seize, and even sink Spanish treasure ships in the Caribbean. He found many ships to attack, and some of them were Spanish.

In 1808 or 1809, he established a headquarters south of New Orleans at Barataria on Barataria Bay, from which he controlled the approaches to New Orleans from the south, and had free access to the Caribbean.

Lafitte established a couple of legitimate businesses in New Orleans, including a blacksmith shop. These, however, were fronts for the real businesses. He sold goods stolen from the ships he captured. He also engaged in the slave trade.

At the beginning of the nineteenth century, the United States outlawed the importation of slaves, but slaves seized from smugglers were sold legally at auction. Many enterprising businessmen arranged for slaves to be smuggled in, but turned the smugglers over to authorities. The reward to the businessmen for this betrayal were the slaves seized. It was then proper and legal to sell them.

Lafitte avoided this by selling the slaves at auction in New Orleans. Although illegal, the governor and government of New Orleans ignored this. Too many influential plantation owners needed the slaves. This trade never caused Lafitte much trouble, but did fill his coffers with treasure.

During these years, Lafitte would sail off by himself for short periods. It was understood that he buried chests full of gold coins, jewels, and other valuables taken during the raids or gained through the sales held in New Orleans. Lafitte didn't trust the banks or all of the men who followed him.

Some of these caches have been found. Treasure hunters on the shore of Long Beach, Mississippi recovered $45,000. A cache of nearly $50,000 was found near Bayou La Batre, Alabama. Another cache of $41,000 was discovered on Gardner Island, Louisiana. The largest find was made on the bank of Bayou Chico near Pensacola, when more than $60,000 in gold and silver coins, all dated before 1804, were recovered by the lucky treasure hunter.

Treasure hunters speculate that all these caches were hidden by Lafitte during his private outings. The amount buried is almost the same, all the coins found date between 1765 and 1803, and the caches were all along the Gulf Coast. Lafitte was the pirate operating in that area at that time. It seems logical that these small treasures belonged to him.

It must be noted that he made many such trips. He apparently stashed treasure where he could get at it easily. He also was gathering gold, silver, jewels, and other valuables at a surprising rate, given the times.

All during this period, Lafitte was operating in the open with authorities looking the other way. However, in January 1811, there was a slave uprising in southern Louisiana. Governor W.C.C. Claiborne tried to blame Lafitte, claiming that the slaves he had brought into the area were the ones who talked of revolt. Without that spark there would have been no uprising.

Claiborne ordered Captain Andrew Holmes to select a group of soldiers and arrest the pirates living in Barataria. He wanted Lafitte and his brother, Pierre, hanged for their crimes.

Lafitte, however, wasn't around to be arrested. He had learned of the plan and was in command of his best ship, the *Pride*. He was searching for the *Independence*, which had sailed from Salem, Mississippi with a treasure of nearly $300,000 in gold.

The ship was found, boarded, and the treasure and other valuable cargo stolen. The crew was killed and the ship set on fire. Lafitte wanted no witnesses to the crime.

On the voyage back to Barataria, they stopped briefly while Lafitte and his brother rowed ashore to hide the gold coins. All that is known is that this happened somewhere between Biloxi and Pass Christian.

Lafitte thought that would be the end of it. Instead, they had made a bigger mistake than believing the *Independence* was Spanish. There was one survivor who had escaped the slaughter and the fire. Captain Williams, master of the *Independence*, hid while the pirates killed the crew. Once they sailed away, he fled from hiding, fought his way through the flames, and lashed himself to a floating hatch cover. A French merchant ship rescued him and took him to New Orleans.

Within hours of learning the fate of the *Independence*, Lafitte and his brother had been arrested by authorities and jailed. To make it worse, if possible, not only was Captain Williams sure about the identities of the pirates, but some of the cargo found in Lafitte's possession was identified as that from the *Independence*.

But Lafitte was not without influence of his own. Lafitte was visited by a lawyer and the district attorney. Bail was set at twelve thousand dollars and within hours of his arrest, Lafitte was free again.

The trial was held; Williams told his story and identified the various items seized as having come from his ship. None of that bothered Lafitte. He forfeited the bond by not showing for the trial. Claiborne offered a reward of one thousand dollars for his capture.

Lafitte was back at sea. During the next several months he raided throughout the Caribbean. Each time he seized a treasure, he buried it immediately. The *Santa Elena* contributed four million dollars in gold and jewels. The treasure was buried near Jefferson Island.

The *Reya del Mar* held only half a million dollars, but Lafitte stole it anyway. It was reported to be buried somewhere near or on Pecan Island.

The *Laguna Roja* was seized. Lafitte stole the $1.25 million in silver and buried it, as was his habit, somewhere in the Isles Dernieres.

Lafitte then returned to Lousiana. Prior to January 20, 1814, notices were posted throughout New Orleans that more than four hundred slaves would be auctioned on that day. Claiborne could not ignore it, even though many plantation owners would be at the auction. He sent a force of dragoons to arrest Lafitte, but once again the pirate was alerted. He dispatched a group of his own men to ambush the soldiers. A revenue inspector was killed in the ambush, as were a couple of the soldiers. Now the governor had to act.

Claiborne ordered Captain Walker Gilbert to find and arrest Lafitte. He failed to find him, but did find Pierre who, outnumbered by the soldiers, surrendered.

Lafitte tried once again to post bail for his brother, but this time nothing could be worked out. Claiborne was too angry and Lafitte had pushed him much too far. His attempts to pay bail failed and his brother remained in jail.

While all this was going on, two British naval officers visited Lafitte at his headquarters in Barataria and recognized its strategically placed importance. With Lafitte's help, the British officers believed they could launch a successful attack on New Orleans.

They offered Lafitte thirty thousand dollars, which wasn't much considering how many caches holding that much or more

Lafitte had hidden. More important than the money was a captain's commission in the British navy.

Lafitte asked for time to think about it. When the British were gone, Lafitte informed Claiborne that the British had propositioned him. Lafitte hoped that he could use the information to free his brother.

Claiborne and his cronies decided that Lafitte was the real threat to New Orleans, not the British. When Lafitte broke his brother out of prison, it was too much for them. On September 11, 1814, an attack was launched against Lafitte's stronghold on Barataria. The assault failed because Lafitte and the majority of his pirates were at sea. Only Lafitte's artillery officer, Dominique You, and seventy-five men were captured. Lafitte lost about three-quarters of a million dollars in supplies and captured booty. His headquarters were burned to the ground. The majority of his men and all his ships were at sea so they escaped the assault.

Lafitte continued his piracy. He stopped and looted Spanish, American, and French ships. Treasure hunters estimate that Lafitte stole two and a half million dollars in gold, silver, and jewels during this short period. The majority of the treasure was buried on Padre Island, the scene of college spring break these days.

The British attack on New Orleans hadn't been forgotten. Even with the War of 1812 winding down, communications were so slow that the British pushed forward their plans. Lafitte, through his system of spies, learned about the attack and reported the intelligence to Andrew Jackson, the man sent to defend New Orleans.

Lafitte offered to help Jackson, supplying him with equipment and ammunition Jackson didn't have. In return, Lafitte asked that his incarcerated men be released. Jackson agreed to the terms and when the British attacked on January 8, 1815, Jackson's troops broke the British assault. Jackson lived up to his end of the bargain, granting the pardons to Lafitte and his men.

Claiborne, however, didn't see it that way. He refused to return the booty that had been seized during the attack on Barataria. Lafitte realized that Claiborne would never be happy until he was dead. He shifted his operations once, and then moved on to Haiti. The Haitian government was no more thrilled to have Lafitte in residence than Claiborne had been. He was ordered to leave as soon as he could.

Lafitte's fallback plan was to join forces with another pirate, Louis Aury, on Galveston Island, near the present-day town of Galveston, Texas. Unfortunately, Aury had joined with a Mexican pirate and had moved into Mexico. That left Lafitte in possession of the island.

By 1818, Lafitte had built a pirate kingdom on Galveston Island. With more than a thousand men and quite a few ships, he raided the entire Caribbean. All during this time, Lafitte continued to bury treasure along the coasts. But none of it was going to last.

In the fall of 1818, a dangerous hurricane struck the island. Lafitte and his brother escaped to one of his ships, the *Maison Rouge*. They rode out the hurricane but when they returned to the island, they found the headquarters destroyed. Hundreds of the pirates had been killed in the tidal surge caused by the hurricane.

Before he could rebuild, an American gunboat arrived, and the officer in charge informed Lafitte that he would not be allowed to rebuild on American soil. Although Lafitte might technically have been in Mexico, he agreed, as long as he was left alone until he could find another base.

During the next several months, Lafitte raided, capturing the *Hampton Queen*, stealing and then burying nearly three quarters of a million dollars on Matagorda Island.

Lafitte also captured the merchant ship *Helen Fry*. He took one and a half million in treasure from it. According to the records, he captured the ship at the mouth of the Sabine River, and then buried that treasure somewhere on the sandy shore of Sabine Lake.

This marked the real end to Lafitte's piracy. After the demise of the merchant ship, two of his most trusted men, Desfarges and Johnston, were captured, tried, and hanged in May 1820. Worse than that, however, was the death of his brother in an ambush set by Mexican authorities. Lafitte didn't recover from that blow.

The story of Lafitte fades away after that. He apparently boarded one of his ships and sailed away. No one seems to know what happened to him. One encyclopedia claims that he died around 1825.

Lafitte left treasures buried all along the Gulf Coast. Some might have been recovered by his associates, but often no one knew where the treasures were but Lafitte. The records show that of the millions and he took and cached, only a few have ever been found.

Corroboration has been discovered after the fact. After the death of his first wife, Lafitte married the young daughter of a French family in Louisiana. She was injured when American forces destroyed his fortress at Barataria. Her injuries were so severe that Lafitte's surgeon could do nothing for her and she died shortly afterward.

Lafitte buried her, and two chests, not far from her grave, on Matagorda Island. One contained her personal possessions, including a music box that had come from Paris. The other contained treasure.

A Texas treasure hunter, Dr. Joseph Wooten, found a map that showed approximately where the two chests were buried. Wooten knew that Lafitte didn't draw maps, so he was uninterested. He learned, however, that on this expedition, Lafitte had been accompanied by one of his top lieutenants. He might have drawn the map.

Using the map, Wooten set out to find the treasure. He spent two years—1913 and 1914—searching Matagorda for the chests. Although he didn't find the chest filled with treasure, he did find the one containing Lafitte's dead wife's possessions. Wooten took them to Port O'Connor, Texas, and sold them to collectors for something around fifty thousand dollars.

The other chest, the one with the treasure, has not been found; at least it has not been reported to have been found. There is the very real possibility that Lafitte's lieutenant, the man who drew the map, returned later and took the treasure for himself. Otherwise, why draw a map?

Historians and treasure hunters believe that between $20 million and $100 million is buried in various locations along the Gulf Coast. Some of those treasures contain gold and silver that was worth several million dollars in the early eighteenth century. And any coins minted prior to 1804 would be worth many times their face value. A treasure with a face value of $50,000 in gold coins might be worth ten or twenty times that to collectors.

So many stories of buried treasures are without foundation. So many are just rumors or theories, but with Lafitte there is solid information that the treasures are out there. All that is needed is a little perseverance and a great deal of luck.

12

STAGECOACH GOLD

—

TEXAS

IN THE MID-1960S, MINERAL Wells, Texas was the home of the Army's Primary Helicopter School. Helicopter pilots, almost every one of them, were sent on to one of two other centers to finish their training, and eventually found their way to Vietnam.

Mineral Wells sits in Palo Pinto County about fifty miles to the west of Fort Worth. It has run through bust and boom and when the military base closed, it could have meant the end of the town. That didn't happen.

Mineral Wells is famous for one other thing and that is the Baker Hotel. At one time it rose from the prairie and dominated the landscape. It could be seen for miles and, from its top floors, a huge expanse of Texas was visible. Right behind it is East Mountain.

In the early days of this century Fort Richardson in Jack County had a major payroll to meet. There were those who knew

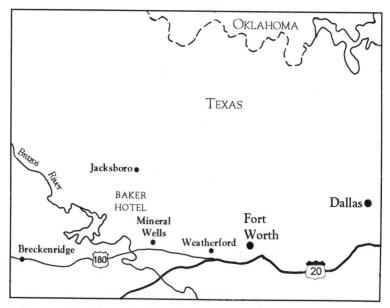

about it, those who knew it was paid in gold, and those who thought they could steal it.

According to J.W. Smith, a butcher who supplied meat to the state penitentiary in Huntsville, Texas, two men tried exactly that. The hold-up, according to a dying convict that Smith knew, had taken place in Jack County near Fort Richardson, but it wasn't the simple task that they had thought. The stage driver and shotgun rider didn't surrender the gold easily. During the shoot-out, one of the robbers was badly wounded, but they did manage to escape with nine boxes of gold.

The problem was that they had too much gold to transport now that one of them was hurt. They managed to get close to Mineral Wells and found a large outcropping of rock that jutted from the side of East Mountain. Behind it was a large cave and the two crooks took refuge inside, hiding the money deep in the interior. The uninjured man bandaged his friend as best he could and then went into town to search for food. Every night he sneaked from the cave, down into the town for whiskey and food and, once in a while, female companionship.

Although his friend was improving, he was unable to take care of himself. He lay in the darkness during the day, sometimes delirious from fever. But the cave was cool and the nights cold and the man was slowly getting better.

One night, while in town, the healthy robber was arrested, then tried, and finally sent on to prison. During the trial for another crime, he never mentioned the gold and he never told anyone about his wounded friend hidden in the cave. He believed that he would get out of prison quickly, and a couple of days one way or the other wouldn't make that much difference to his wounded friend.

Instead of serving a quick sentence in the Palo Pinto County jail as he expected, he found himself on his way to Huntsville in the back of a prison wagon. Even then, he kept his mouth shut, maybe hoping that his friend could survive but believing that he would never leave the cave alive. The gold hidden there would be waiting for him when he finished his prison sentence.

At Huntsville, the man became sick. He knew now that he would never leave the prison alive, so he confided in the one man who had shown him any kindness. That was the butcher, Smith. The man told Smith the story about the robbery, the gold, and the hidden cave in East Mountain.

Smith, having heard many such stories from many other inmates, didn't believe it . . . really. Sometimes the stories were told by convicts who wanted either assistance in escaping or someone to find the treasure to use for new trials or bribe guards and prison officials. Sometimes the stories were told simply as a way of passing the time and entertaining themselves and those around them. Often the stories were illusions, delusions, or just invented for the sheer the joy of storytelling.

If that was all there was to the story, it might have been ignored by serious treasure hunters. An unidentified prisoner telling of nine boxes of gold hidden in a cave isn't much of a trail to follow, especially when there are no names for the robbers. But there is another aspect to the story.

In the mid-1960s, while the Primary Helicopter School was filled with students, one of the men who worked on the Fort Wolters reservation was named Joe, called Indian Joe by everyone there who knew him. He, along with a few friends assigned to the permanent party—that is, the men and women assigned to the base as opposed to the student pilots who were there for only a six month period—were treasure hunters. They had metal detectors, and talked of hidden gold.

But Joe had once been very close to a real treasure and hadn't known it at the time. As a boy, Joe, and a friend, John A. Stamford, explored the cave in East Mountain behind the Baker Hotel. They hadn't gotten very deep into the cave when they found a human skeleton. They took the skull and carried it to the office of Doctors Raines and Bowers.

Several years later, Joe, as a young man, heard the story of the robbery. Excited because he knew that part of the story was true, Joe made plans to return to Mineral Wells with Smith. Both dreamed of nine boxes of gold guarded by a long dead man with a now headless skeleton.

But when they reached Mineral Wells, they found that the natural entrance to the cave had collapsed. They searched the mountain for another entrance, at first convinced there had to be one. When that failed, they planned to dig on the mountain, hoping to hit the original cave. They assumed that it would still be there. Just the entrance was gone.

Their attempts to retrieve the gold failed. Joe, now aware of the whole story, thought of the excitement he had felt at the discovery of the human skeleton with its ragged clothes and rusted old revolver. Those finds had been the treasure of a young boy who didn't think about exploring the cave farther hoping to find more valuable wealth. Instead he invented tales of Indian fights, or desperate men.

There is no evidence that anyone found the gold. Those who knew about it failed to get it. The robber died in prison, and Smith didn't believe until it was too late. Maybe the whole cave collapsed, burying the gold under tons of rock and dirt where no one will ever find it. Maybe, as Joe believed, it was just the entrance that collapsed. Maybe the gold now lies just a few feet from the surface waiting for the right person to stumble across it.

13

JOHN DILLINGER'S LOOT

—

WISCONSIN

STORIES OF HIDDEN WEALTH
always circulate around the exploits of bank robbers. They steal
large amounts of money, but when captured, seem to have little
of it. There are tales that suggest they spend it as fast as they steal
it. And there are tales that they have a stash buried somewhere
to finance an escape or legal defense or a celebration party.

John Dillinger ranged throughout the Midwest during the
Great Depression, robbing dozens of banks. Unlike some of the
others, he had a certain flair, stealing large amounts of money.
While Bonnie and Clyde might steal a thousand or two thousand from a bank, or fifty dollars from a small grocery store or
service station, Dillinger was taking tens of thousands of dollars
in his bank robberies.

That is not to say that Dillinger was anything other than a
cold-blooded killer and a ruthless criminal. The men he was asso-

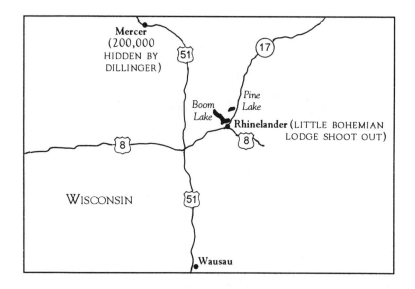

ciated with were as criminal and cold-blooded as Dillinger, often killing for no reason other than the thrill of watching someone die.

Dillinger's last run of freedom began on March 3, 1934, when, using his famous pistol carved from soap, he broke out of the Crown Point, Indiana jail. He headed immediately toward St. Paul, Minnesota to link up with his girlfriend, Billie Frechette. There he began to assemble a new gang to continue his career.

With Baby Face Nelson, among others, Dillinger made his first robbery just three days after breaking out of jail. They hit the Security National Bank and Trust Company in Sioux Falls, South Dakota. They escaped with $49,000 in a white sack.

Ten days later, on March 13, they robbed the First National Bank in Mason City, Iowa. Gang member Eddie Green had learned through friends that the bank held nearly a quarter of a million dollars. While Dillinger stood outside in the street guarding prisoners, and Baby Face Nelson guarded the rear of the bank, Green and John Hamilton were inside, trying to get at all that money.

Cashier Harry Fisher stood inside the bank, locked behind a barred door. Fisher was in with the stacks of money, but told Hamilton that he couldn't unlock the barred door for any of a number of reasons. All he could do was pass the money between the bars to the robber. Fisher grabbed a stack of one dollar bills, handed them through, and then turned back to grab more cash.

Outside, still guarding the prisoners, Dillinger was wounded by an old policeman, John Shipley, who fired down from a third floor window. Dillinger shot back, but Shipley ducked behind the windowsill.

The robbery had been quickly planned to the last second and time finally ran out. Another of the Dillinger gang, Homer Van Meter, who held the stopwatch and counted off the seconds, began yelling, "Let's go!"

With stacks of cash still visible in the vault where the robbers couldn't reach it, though they could see it, they were forced to run. They fled with a car loaded with hostages. Police arrived on the scene to watch as the car carrying the Dillinger gang sped away. They believed a shootout would result in the deaths of the hostages, and refused to give chase. Outside of town, the hostages were set free.

Although Dillinger and his gang didn't get the quarter of a million, records indicate they stole something over $52,000. Hamilton said later that he should have shot the cashier. All that money had been left in the vault where they couldn't get at it because the cashier wouldn't grab the tens and twenties, but insisted on giving him ones.

Dillinger returned to St. Paul and was treated for his minor wound by Dr. N. G. Mortenson, a city health officer. Mortenson recognized Dillinger immediately but didn't call the police, afraid that one of the other gang members would return to kill him.

Others in St. Paul, however, recognized Dillinger and alerted the FBI. Agents R.L. Nalls and R.C. Coulter tracked Dillinger to the Lincoln Court Apartments. On March 31, 1934, they went to arrest him.

Billie Frechette answered the door, telling the agents that her husband was asleep and she wasn't dressed. When they insisted that she open the door for them, she told them to wait. Quietly, she alerted Dillinger that FBI agents were outside.

As the agents stood in the hallway, Van Meter entered the building and began to climb the stairs. Challenged by the FBI men, he said he was just a traveling soap salesman. He told them that his samples were in the car and if they would come with him, he'd prove it to them.

On the first floor, Van Meter whirled suddenly, threatening one of the FBI agents with the pistol pulled from his shoulder holster. The agent reacted quickly, and ran past Van Meter, surprising him. Van Meter didn't fire. Instead, remembering the second agent still upstairs, Van Meter fled, leaving Dillinger behind.

Agent Nalls then walked downstairs to investigate the noise, leaving the way clear for Dillinger. He sprayed the hallway with his machine gun and then ran down the rear stairs with Frechette. Nalls fired at Dillinger once or twice, hitting him in the leg.

St. Paul was suddenly too hot for Dillinger. His friend, Pat Reilly, told him there was a quiet resort in northern Wisconsin, named Little Bohemia, where he could hide out. It wasn't open yet, but they could hole up there without having to worry about being disturbed by the local authorities or vacationers.

From the time that Dillinger broke out of the Crown Point Jail a few weeks earlier, he had pulled two bank robberies netting just over a hundred thousand dollars in cash. That money had been split among the participants and some of it had been spent. Dillinger apparently didn't have a great deal of money with him when he arrived in Little Bohemia.

However, before driving to Rhinelander, Wisconsin, and the Little Bohemia Lodge, he took a side trip into Chicago. Apparently Dillinger visited his lawyer, telling the man to keep certain monies readily available because he would soon be going on a long trip.

Before heading to Rhinelander, Dillinger and Van Meter attacked the police station in Warsaw, Indiana, stealing weapons and bulletproof vests from the armory. From there they drove on to the lodge to rest and plan their next bank robbery.

The FBI and Melvin Purvis, the special agent in charge of the Chicago office, received another tip, this one telling them that Dillinger was hiding out in Wisconsin. With agents from Minnesota and Chicago, Purvis drove to the Little Bohemia Lodge. When everything was ready, Purvis walked to the front of the lodge.

Three men exited about that time, walking calmly to their car. They climbed in as the FBI agents began shouting at them. Inside the car, with the windows rolled up, the men didn't hear the warnings from the FBI. As they pulled away, the FBI, thinking it was Dillinger and members of his gang escaping, opened fire. Eugene Boiseneau, a CCC (Civilian Conservation Core) worker and innocent man, was killed instantly. His two friends were wounded.

The shooting outside alerted Dillinger. Grabbing a large suitcase, Dillinger and his friends ran out the back door. Local legend claims that as Dillinger fled, he stopped long enough to bury the suitcase near a big oak tree and two pines north of the lodge near Highway 51.

Baby Face Nelson, in a separate cabin near the lodge, entered the fight. He fired a few random shots from a window and then ran into the woods. He left his wife behind in the cabin.

All night the FBI, who had finally surrouded the lodge, shot it up, thinking the gangsters were still hiding inside. In the morning after they realized there was no return fire, they entered and found no one of interest except the gangsters' girlfriends who had been hiding in the basement.

Purvis and the FBI were embarrassed over the results of the raid. They had killed an innocent man, wounded two others, and had nothing to show for it. J. Edgar Hoover then issued a shoot-to-kill order on Dillinger and posted a $10,000 reward. Five of the states in which Dillinger had robbed banks offered an additional $10,000 reward.

By July, Dillinger had been traced back to Chicago. Legend has it he was killed outside the Biograph movie theatre on July 22, 1934, three months to the day that he had escaped from the Little Bohemia Lodge. All members of the Dillinger gang assembled after his break from the Crown Point Jail were dead by the end of 1934, the last being Baby Face Nelson, killed in a shootout with the FBI on November 27, 1934.

If Dillinger buried anything near the Little Bohemia Lodge, he never had the chance to recover it. None of his gang members returned to the area before they were killed by police or FBI. Therefore, anything buried by Dillinger probably remains where he left it.

Local legend claims that more than a million dollars in securities are buried 500 yards north of the Little Bohemia Lodge near a big oak and two pine trees. These securities were not part of the loot stolen from various banks, but part of Dillinger's escape fund. Some have speculated that retrieval of the securities is the reason that Dillinger had gone to see his lawyer in Chicago.

There are also legends that Dillinger buried $200,000 not far from Rhinelander, near Mercer, Wisconsin. One source suggests it might be as much as $700,000 in cash. Local residents say that the long periods of freezing weather and frozen ground would preserve the cash if it was buried there. It should still be in fairly good shape.

There are, however, a couple of problems. First, it doesn't seem that Dillinger had the financial resources to bury large amounts of cash. In the days before the Little Bohemia raid, Dillinger had stolen, with his gang, little more than a hundred thousand. He might have secured more when he visited his lawyer in Chicago. The real question is, why bury the money when running from the FBI? It would seem that a large amount of money would make an escape easier.

If Dillinger buried anything upon his escape from the lodge, it is most likely to have been weapons. In January 1934, before the final run, Dillinger and his gang, Harry Pierpont, Charles Makley, Russell Clark, and John Hamilton, among others, headed to Tucson, Arizona. Clark and Makley were arrested when a fire broke out in their hotel and they offered firefighters hundreds of dollars to bring out their suitcases. One of the firemen became suspicious because of the weight. When he opened the suitcase, he found several pistols and a machine gun.

The others were quickly found and arrested as well. The gang was then split, with Dillinger transferred to the Crown Point Jail. It would seem that any money Dillinger had prior to that point was lost or had been spent by him. According to records, the largest single robbery by Dillinger netted just over $75,000.

Other robberies had been blamed on Dillinger, or his gang, or makeshift gangs. For example, the Merchants National Bank in South Bend, Indiana was robbed on June 30, 1934, supposedly by Dillinger, Baby Face Nelson, and Pretty Boy Floyd. The available records suggest that none of them were in Indiana on that date and that none of them participated in the crime. It made better headlines if the Dillinger gang committed the crime rather than a group of unknown locals.

The Rhinelander local legends then suggest that Dillinger buried a suitcase near the lodge during his escape. Local legend says it contained a large amount of cash and securities. However, it seems more likely that if Dillinger buried anything, it was a suitcase containing weapons.

That might not be the treasure that some would want, but a stash of guns in good condition would be worth money to a collector. And if those guns belonged at one time to John Dillinger, they would be worth even more.

14

DUTCH SCHULTZ'S SEVEN MILLION DOLLARS

—

NEW YORK

DURING PROHIBITION IN THE 1920s, and into the Depression of the 1930s, there was one group who made lots of money. They provided the alcohol that the public demanded, and used the money gained to finance gambling, prostitution, and even drugs. The gangsters of that era earned millions of dollars. They spread their wealth around, spending lavishly. They owned summer houses, bulletproof cars, and anything else they could think of. The money rolled in and although they were subject to the same tax laws as everyone else, they didn't bother with them.

The exception that proves this rule was Arthur Flegenheimer, known as Dutch Schultz. He was described as the cheapest guy who ever lived. He didn't even want to spend the two pennies it

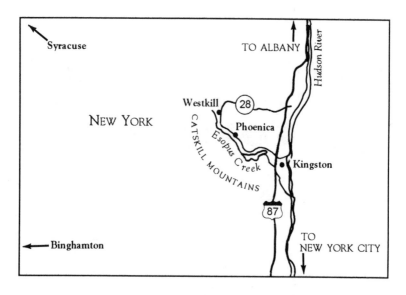

cost for a newspaper. He had millions and he wanted to keep it all for himself.

Schultz was born in 1902 and grew up in the Bronx. He apparently did go through four grades at Public School No. 12. Shortly after his father deserted him in 1916, when Schultz was fourteen, Schultz began to go "bad."

Eventually he was running his own speakeasies, bringing in liquor from Canada, and creating his own, bad-tasting beer. He recruited others to protect his turf. In the course of his short career, he was responsible for 135 murders. It was his unreasonable attitude, and his desire to kill then-district attorney, Thomas Dewey, that led to his own death in 1935. His fellow mobsters believed Dewey too powerful and thought that if he was killed, there would be no rest. If Schultz killed Dewey, the entire weight of the government would fall on them.

Just before he decided he wanted to kill Dewey, like so many others, Schultz was arrested for income tax evasion. Not sure of the outcome of the trial, Schultz had a steel box created by a Bronx ironworker. Schultz decided to hide some of his wealth.

According to various witnesses, including Lulu Rosenkrantz, Dixie Davis, Otto Beiderman, Abe Landau, and Marty Krompier, Schultz filled the steel box with thousand dollar bills, diamonds, gold coins, and other valuables. They estimated that the box contained about seven million dollars.

Schultz and Rosenkrantz loaded the trunk into Schultz's Packard and then drove to upstate New York. They drove into the Catskill Mountains. Approaching Phoenicia, they stopped near a stand of pine trees on the bank of Esopus Creek. There they buried the steel box.

Schultz was not convicted of income tax evasion. He did not return to reclaim his buried wealth. He trusted no one and probably believed the millions were as safe there as anywhere else. There is no evidence that Schultz ever tried to recover the steel box.

Schultz never told anyone where the box was buried. Rosenkrantz, however, did talk. He drew a crude map with instructions on how to find the loot. The map showed the pine trees with a cross marked at the base of one of the trees. The road to Phoenicia was on the map, as well as a one-story shack with the label "Lodging for hunters and fishermen."

Rosenkrantz didn't live as long as Schultz. He had given his map to Marty Krompier. He didn't want to search for the money while Schultz was alive, but he thought enough of the map to keep it in his wallet.

Krompier wasn't as cautious as the others and let it be known that he had the map to Schultz's millions. He was killed in a barbershop by one of Gurrah Shapiro's friends. They demanded the Schultz map, but then opened fire, killing him before he could say anything to them. They stole the map from the body, but apparently were unable to understand it without knowing a little more about the landmarks.

Gurrah searched for the treasure a couple of times but he didn't find much. He quickly lost interest and the map disappeared shortly after that.

The important thing here is that there were witnesses to Schultz's burying the treasure. There are no indications that it was ever recovered. Those who could have found it were afraid of Schultz. The man with him when the treasure was hidden died before Schultz. The others waited until after Schultz himself was dead, but they didn't find the steel box. The map and a key were stolen and then lost.

Somewhere along the Esopus Creek, near a stand of pine trees (or the remains of those trees), along the road that leads to Phoenicia, is a buried steel box holding gold, negotiable securities, gold coins, and jewelry. It was worth seven million dollars in the 1930s. There are no reports that it was found, and those thousand dollar bills, if they had suddenly turned up in circulation, would have been proof the loot was recovered. So the treasure waits, hidden in a steel box, probably worth much more than the rumored seven million.

PART IV

REAL CACHES
OF
BURIED TREASURE

15

MILITARY
GOLD BARS

—

PENNSYLVANIA

THE TREASURE IS MADE UP OF
28 gold bars, each weighing about 50 pounds and worth $10,000
in 1863. Total value of the treasure, in 1863, was just over a
quarter of a million dollars. On today's market, with gold worth
hundreds of dollars an ounce, the value is estimated at several
million.

Only half of one bar has ever been found. An official court of
inquiry tried to establish the fate of the guards and the gold after
they were lost. In other words, this is one treasure story that has
been documented by the United States government. The location of the treasure is well known, though the area to be searched
is fairly large.

The gold seems to have been mined in California and then
shipped to the east. Before the Civil War, gold was transported by
ship around Cape Horn, a long and sometimes dangerous trip. By

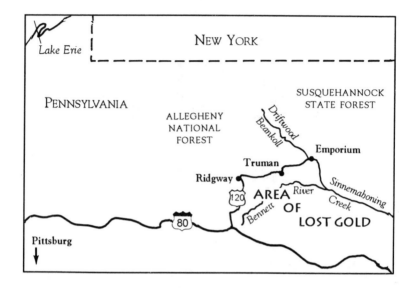

1861, the gold was being sent overland to the railroad in St. Louis, and then on to the Mint in Philadelphia by train and riverboat.

Even this route had its dangers, first from hostile Indians and then from Southern sympathizers. The normal dangers of thieves and train robbers were always present, but the federal government needed money to support its growing budget. By the end of 1861, the Civil War had begun and the cost of fighting was growing daily.

In 1863, another shipment of gold had been sent east and had arrived in Wheeling, West Virginia. A young lieutenant, John Castleton, was given command of the wagon train carrying the gold. His orders were simple: Take the gold to the Mint in Philadelphia. This was just weeks before Federal and Rebel forces clashed at Gettysburg.

Castleton was born into a family of famous military men and attended West Point. He resigned from West Point after only two years and joined a volunteer cavalry unit, organized by his uncle, to fight in the Mexican War. His short and undistinguished career should have been ended by a severe hip wound and malaria, but was not.

Rather than a discharge after his recovery, he was assigned as a clerk to various military outposts. His thrill of Army life eroded and he became a bitter and inept officer. He took an extended leave and settled in Pike County, Missouri.

In 1855, he joined a band of raiders, known as Jennison's Jayhawkers, who attacked proslavery towns in both Kansas and Missouri. When the Civil War began six years later, he reported to General Price for duty in St. Louis. He was eventually sent to the Army staff headquarters in Cincinnati.

By June 1863, Castleton found himself in Wheeling, West Virginia and was given orders to escort two wagons to the Mint in Philadelphia. He was given eight cavalrymen for his escort, and he was to avoid any and all contact with the enemy. Hidden in false bottoms of the wagons were twenty-eight gold ingots that had arrived from the gold fields in California.

Castleton was assigned a sergeant as his second in command. Sergeant Mike O'Rourke was an uneducated man who had been raised in various river towns. He was wanted by several law enforcement agencies for brawling. O'Rourke had eventually joined the Jayhawkers where he and Castleton became friends.

Of the others assigned to the tiny command, limited information is available. One of them, a nasty man named Connors, had served in the Army of the Potomac, been wounded in combat, and was assigned limited duty. Unfortunately, he knew O'Rourke and the two men hated one another.

With the guard detail assembled, they left Wheeling and met a riverboat, the River Queen, where a dummy load, as well as the gold, was loaded onto the wagons. They then traveled east, around Pittsburgh, using back roads, avoiding towns and roving enemy patrols.

During the trip, Castleton had became very ill when his malaria flared up. With O'Rourke, he rode into Ridgeway, Pennsylvania to buy Peruvan Bark to treat his illness. The town's inhabitants were unfriendly and believed that the two men were "drafters," that is, men who recruited with a rifle or a pistol, rather than regular recruiting practices.

Castleton and O'Rourke escaped the town after a fight, but that night several of the town's men attacked the camp. They tried to run off the horses, but Castleton's little band drove the attackers away instead.

At dawn, they broke camp, detoured around the town, and headed to the east, along what would later become Route 120 in central Pennsylvania. Eventually they reached St. Mary's, where they met a man named Richardson, who had been mentioned in their original orders. Richardson was to guide them through the mountains to the area of West Branch. Richardson, however, wouldn't go with them. He gave them a map drawn about twenty years earlier that showed a road that would take them through the mountains.

This time, possibly because of Richardson, the townspeople were friendly, selling the soldiers the supplies they needed and assisting them in repairing the wagons. They rested two days before moving off to the east, following a road that was nearly invisible.

After two days, Castleton, still sick and riding in one of the wagons, tried to hire a guide. A man identified as Joe, who claimed he could guide them to their destination, wanted an advance payment to buy a pair of new boots. Castleton agreed and Joe disappeared, promising to return.

In the morning, however, Joe didn't reappear. O'Rourke went to find him. Joe didn't have new boots, but did have a hangover.

Joe told O'Rourke he was sick and remembered nothing about a bargain to guide any soldiers through the mountains to Philadephia.

The party left the camp with a reluctant Joe and began to work their way along a road next to a stream known at one time as Brunner Brook. After a day's march, they stopped again in a small clearing. Joe tried to talk himself out of the camp, wanting to visit an area where he had trapped in the past. Castleton made it clear that Joe would remain in camp with the soldiers. They weren't going to let him fade into the landscape again.

They were now within ten or fifteen miles of the Sinnemahoning River. According to the map, and to Joe, they should reach it within two days. Neither Castleton nor O'Rourke trusted their guide, O'Rourke suggesting that they double-check him against the compass and the map. Castleton, realizing the situation was out of hand, asked O'Rourke to take overall command if he became too sick to do it.

That night it rained and Castleton became sicker. Joe convinced O'Rourke to remain where they were for the day. The following day was bright and clear and they pushed off with Castleton watching their progress on his map.

Joe, however, seemed confused. He didn't know which road was the one they wanted. Castleton used his compass and checked the map, finally selecting a road that ran to the west. But after half a day's march, the road faded away in a small clearing.

They again made camp and tried to determine what to do next. They questioned Joe carefully and he admitted that he had never been in that area before. Joe thought there was an old cabin off to the east somewhere. If he could get to the cabin, he was sure that he could find the river.

Connors, who had been fairly quiet up to that point, finally spoke up. Joe was a liar, according to Connors, and the only intelligent course was to abandon the wagons now. Without them, they would be able to make better time, and could find their way out of the forest. But they couldn't make any time if they had to detour around swamps and rocky cliffs dragging the wagons with them.

Instead, Castleton decided they would stay on the top of the ridge where the timber was sparse. But the problem wasn't solved; they were still lost. Castleton just got sicker, and without him, O'Rourke was no leader. Command fell to Connors by default.

Connors decided that they would have to abandon the wagons, and use the canvas covers on the gold ingots to create packs. They would carry the gold out of the woods on the mules. Castleton, sick as he was, would have to be left behind and two men would stay with him. Connors would leave in the morning with the majority of the soldiers.

But, in the morning, Castleton was feeling better and decided that Connors's plan was unworkable. He was not going to let the gold out of his sight. The new plan was for Castleton and five of the men to head south as fast as they could. Connors and two others would head southeast on foot to try to find help.

Castleton gave Connors his written orders as well as a document allowing Connors to requisition men and supplies for the patrol. As he left, Connors heard Castleton and O'Rourke arguing about carrying all the gold or burying part of it where they were. That was the last that anyone ever saw or heard of Castleton and his group.

Ten days later Connors returned with a group of men from Lock Haven. He found the wagons but the men were gone. Several trails led from the campsite, and Connors believed that the party had split up for some reason. They searched the immediate area but found nothing. Connors called off the search after a short time and returned to Lock Haven.

The War Department believed that Castleton and O'Rourke had conspired to steal the gold bars. Both men were also wanted by the Army for desertion in the face of the enemy, a very serious charge considering that the Army of Northern Virginia had invaded Pennsylvania about the time Castleton had entered the state. The charges, however, were suspended, pending further investigation, probably because of pressure applied by Castleton's rather influential family.

Connors suspected that Joe, the hired guide, had met with bushwackers who planned to steal the gold. The Army, however, suspected that Connors had something to do with the disappearance of the gold and the soldiers. They questioned him carefully and at length, trying to learn the truth. They couldn't break his story, they could discover no evidence that he was lying, but they refused to discharge him.

At the inquest held at the end of the war to determine the fate of the soldiers and the gold, Connors said, "We left camp at daybreak and struck out through the timber east toward the rising sun. We traveled light. We carried no arms and only short rations for two days, for food was getting scarce.

"I gave Billy a knife and told him to mark trees so we could find our way back if necessary. From a rocky outcrop, I saw the ridge sloped down to the east, and soon the downslope became apparent and shortly after midday we came to a large spring, and here we stopped and ate a scanty meal.

"We followed a brook that started from the spring southeast and late that evening we came to where it joined a larger stream, Hicks Run. We crossed this stream and found a faint footpath. Here we spent the night.

"During the next forenoon Sam, who was the most clumsy person I ever saw, stepped on a rolling stone and sprained his ankle and we had to walk on each side of him to help him hobble along and it was awkward for the three of us to walk abreast in the narrow path.

"Late that afternoon, we came to an old deserted cabin standing on a bluff near the stream. I left Billy and Sam at the cabin with most of the food, and went on alone until it was too dark to travel.

"About ten o'clock the next morning I came to a wide valley and a large stream, which I took to be the Sinnemahoning, and there on the flats was a house and clearing. I hurried across a field of corn and potatoes and saw a woman and children, but when I called out to them they ran to the house, closed the door, and the woman screamed that if I didn't go away, she would shoot at me.

"I didn't blame her much. I hadn't shaved in a week, and there were some pretty rough characters roaming in the woods. There was no use hanging around there, so I went on downstream and an hour or so later I came to a cluster of buildings on a flat at the junction of a stream coming in from the north.

"As I neared the settlement, suddenly I felt faint and dizzy, and the next thing I remember, I woke up in a bed. My hostess, a Mrs. Walker, told me I had run a high fever and had been delirious for 48 hours. She had found the papers Castleton gave me and had sent them to the Army post at Lock Haven by her half grown son. Her husband and two brothers were with McClelland in Virginia.

"I recovered fast, and two days later, three soldiers showed up and said a larger rescue party was on its way. I was worried about Castleton and his men, as much as I disliked some of them. They must be starving by now.

"Two days later the rescue party arrived, two wagons loaded with supplies, a pack train of mules, and six men. The officer in charge, Captain Davis, seemed to be a competent man. He agreed with me, assuming the Castleton party had made some progress to the south, we would take a course to intercept them, rather than to follow by backtrail, back to the place where I had left the Castleton party. Just as we were about to start, who should come blundering down the trail, but Sam and Billy. It was a wonder they hadn't starved or got lost, they were the most useless men I ever saw. We sent them down to the settlement, and we started up Hicks Run to the forks and then followed a logging road to the top of the ridge between the two branches. Once on the ridge we searched for signs of Castleton and his men.

"I was lost most of the time but Davis and his men seemed to know the country well. Moving north two days later, we found abandoned wagons where I had left the Castleton party. The trail led off to the southwest, and it seemed to Davis and his woodsmen that the party had split up and wandered off in several directions. We couldn't find any of them, and finally Davis called off the search and we went back to Lock Haven."

The Army officers who made up the board of inquiry didn't know if they should believe Connors or not. There were some problems with his story, and he couldn't find the cabin that he had claimed he had stayed in. As a result, he was not discharged from the Army, and he was not allowed to return to the area. He eventually died in the West.

The Army then turned the investigation over to Allan Pinkerton, who provided intelligence to the Army during the Civil War. He also founded the Pinkerton Detective Agency, whose logo was an all seeing human eye, which gave rise to the term "Private Eye."

Pinkerton suggested that he needed secrecy to find the lost men and the gold. If the civilians learned that a shipment of gold had been lost, they would all be out searching for the treasure. Release of the information would inhibit his investigation.

Pinkerton's men moved into the Sinnemahoning area, posing as prospectors. Nothing was found until the summer of 1865, when two detectives, Donivan and Dugan, found half a gold ingot buried under a pine stump. It looked as if it had been hacked in half by an ax, which might have meant the missing gold had been stolen and the loot divided.

There are also stories that the two detectives found two and a half bars of the missing gold. Either way, the discovery of only a small part of the treasure is interesting. The fact that one bar had been cut does suggest a division of the gold into shares, rather than a splitting of the load to be carried on by individuals to the Philadelphia Mint.

In 1866, other Pinkerton detectives found two mules that had been part of Castleton's livestock. An old man, living in Chase Run, didn't want to talk about how he had acquired the mules, but finally admitted that he had found them.

Ten years later, a survey crew on the Elk–Cameron County line found scattered bones near the Bell's Branch of Dent's Run. Based on the skulls, they identified the remains as human. They gathered the bones and buried them. There is no reason to assume this find had anything to do with the lost gold or Castleton's missing men.

The official search for the gold was abandoned in 1871. The Army then opened a full-scale investigation of the incident. They recalled Connors, but Billy and Sam had been killed in the Civil War. Connors, interviewed at the Carlisle Barracks, stuck to his original story.

After the inquiry, Connors returned to his posts in the West. When drinking, he would sometimes hint that he knew more about the lost gold than he had told the Board of Inquiry. That might not be anything more than a drunk soldier spinning a tale to entertain his buddies and convince them to buy him drinks. He died of pneumonia in Yuma, Arizona in 1886. He was still in the Army at the time and there is no evidence he was a rich man.

The only indication that any of the soldiers with Castleton survived was a rumor that surfaced after the war. A man who looked a great deal like Sergeant O'Rourke was reported to have served in a Union guerrilla unit commanded by Major Terrill. He went by the name Bryam. Of course that is speculation, and certainly doesn't prove anything. Besides, if O'Rourke had survived and the gold had been split up, why would O'Rourke risk his life fighting the war?

There are indications that the Army reopened the investigation as late as 1941. The Army record proved that the gold had been shipped and it proved that it never arrived at its destination. The men who had been guarding it, with few exceptions, disappeared completely. They may have died waiting for rescue, or they might have stolen the gold for themselves killing Castleton. The only thing known for certain is that the gold ingots, along with the guards, disappeared almost completely.

The location of the treasure is fairly well known. It is a small area in Cameron County in central Pennsylvania. The stream mentioned, the West Branch of Hick's Run, is in the southwestern corner of the county. Highway 120 runs from Ridgeway to Emporium. The site where Connors claimed that he had last seen Castleton, O'Rourke, and the gold is a small area south of Truman and west of Cameron between the West Branch and East Branch of Hick's Run.

There is one other point to be made. If Connors conspired to steal the gold, why did he remain in the Army? In that era men deserted regularly, moved to another part of the country, and lived their lives without fear of arrest. So many men deserted that no one really cared. The fact that he remained in the Army, serving in the West, suggests that he did not steal the gold nor did he know who did.

Only a small part of the treasure, either a half ingot, or two and a half ingots, have been recovered. Given today's prices, what is left out there is a treasure worth more than eight or nine million dollars.

Because of the documentation, because it is well known that the gold did exist, and because there is no indication that anyone has found it, this is one of the better treasure stories.

16

KELLY'S BLUFF GOLD

—

IOWA

JUST BEFORE HIS DEATH, THE man known around Dubuque, Iowa only as Kelly, wrote a note to the world. "If you want my gold, you can look for it."

According to the local legends, Kelly arrived in Dubuque in 1832. No one knows why he settled in Dubuque and no one paid much attention to him when he did. He dressed in shabby clothes and old boots. He explored the town on the Mississippi River and then moved to the bluffs behind the present location of St. Raphael's Cathedral.

Kelly's prospecting didn't lead him to gold. Instead, he staked a claim and began mining lead ore. He'd found a rich vein that, ironically, did produce gold. He shipped his lead ore out of Dubuque and received gold coins in payment. It was one of the richest lead mines in the county.

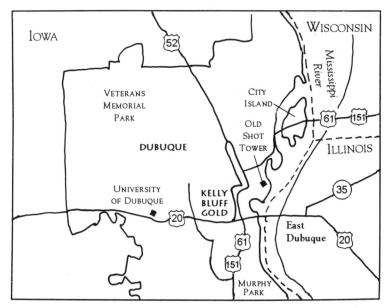

There were those in Dubuque who watched Kelly carefully and knew that he was raking in large payments for his lead from back East. They also knew that he didn't trust banks. They believed that he had buried his gold somewhere on his claim. They searched for it at night, or when Kelly wasn't there, but Kelly had hidden his gold well because no one found it.

In 1847, Kelly left his lead mine to travel with a shipment down the Mississippi. The shipment, valued at $15,000, was to be taken to New Orleans on a barge and then on to New York by ship. The barge never made it to New Orleans, sinking en route. Kelly lost the entire shipment.

Kelly, however, continued on to New York, apparently hoping to collect the insurance. His conduct and his clothing attracted local attention. One day Kelly decided he was being followed by a man who wanted to steal his money belt. In an attempt to escape, Kelly jumped on a streetcar, only to be followed by the stranger. Convinced that the robbery would soon take place, Kelly shot and killed the man.

Kelly was arrested, but in a preliminary hearing he was ordered confined at an asylum in Utica, New York. Apparently his strange actions, his strange dress, and his refusal to assist in his own defense convinced the authorities that he wasn't a murderer, but was insane. There is no record that he was ever brought to trial. He remained in Utica for seven years before he managed to escape. He returned immediately to Dubuque, refusing to ever leave his property again.

It is estimated that Kelly managed to hide about $50,000 in gold coins in various locations on his property. Over the years, others have found treasures valued at $10,000, $1,800, and $500 in gold coins. There are those who claim that more than $36,000 is still buried along the bluffs.

One other point should be made. Kelly died in 1859, just a couple of years after his return from New York. The legend has it that he buried gold coins. While the face value of that treasure is considerable, a glance at any coin book shows that many gold coins minted before 1859 are important to collectors. Most are worth more than $1,000 and some as much as fifty or sixty times that. In today's gold coin market, the value of the treasure to a coin collector might easily exceed a million. Although value to collectors is pure speculation, when dealing with treasure it is something that must be considered.

Kelly's Bluff rises behind Second and Bluff Streets in Dubuque. The location of Kelly's claim is well known. For years the site has been searched by hunters using metal detectors, picks, and shovels, and clues that have been handed down from generation to generation.

There has been no indication that anyone has located the bulk of Kelly's hidden gold. It might still be sitting there, near downtown Dubuque, where it will take nothing more than a little luck to find. This is one of the few treasures that is fairly well pinpointed and fairly well documented. And, as far as it is known, the bulk of it is still there for the taking.

17

CUSTER'S LOST GOLD

—

MONTANA

IN THE APPENDIX FOLLOWING this chapter there is a report that the Seventh Cavalry rode to their deaths at the Little Big Horn with their pockets filled with money. They had been paid after they left Fort Abraham Lincoln. Most of the money was lost because the Indian victors didn't recognize it as anything other than colored paper. Two Cheyenne braves might have recovered some of the cash, hiding it near the battlefield to be retrieved later.

Stories of large amounts of cash, gold, and silver carried by Custer's regiment have circulated for years. Historians and experts have suggested that Custer carried nothing of extreme value and tales of lost treasure are a myth.

However, there is one documented story of a shipment of gold that left Bozeman, Montana and was to be delivered to Fort Abraham Lincoln in the Dakota Territory. The shipment left about the time Custer was riding into Montana. The day after

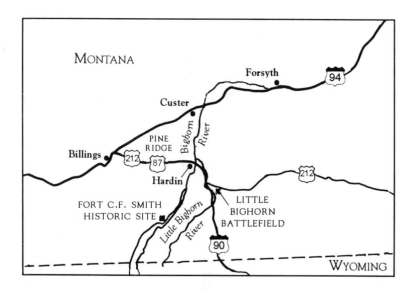

Custer and five companies of the regiment died, the men with the gold were beginning to wonder if they would live long enough to deliver it. All of the Montana Territory was alive with hostile Indians.

For decades after the battle, it was assumed that Gil Longworth and his two armed guards had been attacked and killed by Indians shortly after they had hidden the gold in the Pryor Mountains. After all, that was where their bodies had been found and that was where the remains of their burned out wagon were located.

The location of the search changed after the discoverey of the log of the *Far West*, a riverboat that looms large in the stories of the massacre at the Little Bighorn. The boat was the scene of the last meeting of officers to plan the campaign against the Sioux and Cheyenne. After the battle, the wounded who had been with Major Marcus A. Reno were transported on the

Far West. Most accounts of the history of the battle mention the role of the riverboat.

Captain Marsh, of the *Far West*, had been ordered to meet General Alfred Terry at the confluence of the Bighorn and the Little Bighorn Rivers. Marsh, however, was not familiar with the river. It was his first trip upriver and somehow he missed the rendezvous and sailed on past.

Marsh went, according to the captain's logbook, fifteen or twenty miles beyond where he was to meet General Terry. The sun was setting, and Marsh didn't want to return on a river with which he was unfamiliar. There was just too much danger. Marsh decided to tie up near a wagon crossing.

Longworth arrived not long after Marsh had set his anchor. He climbed aboard to tell Marsh that the Montana Territory was swarming with hostile Sioux. Although neither man knew, Custer and more than half his regiment were already dead. Reno, along with Captain Frederick Benteen and the remainder of the Seventh, were trapped on a hilltop fighting for their lives. For the moment, the Sioux and Cheyenne controlled Montana.

It was the gold that worried Longworth. He knew that he would never make it to Dakota. It was too far and there were too many warriors in the way. Longworth wanted Marsh to store the gold on the *Far West*. That way, it would eventually reach its destination, and Longworth could return with the guards to Bozeman. Marsh reluctantly agreed.

The gold was transferred to the riverboat, and Longworth returned to the wagon. They wasted no time getting out of the region and headed back to Bozeman as fast as they could go.

Marsh didn't like having the gold on the boat. As darkness fell Marsh, along with his top officers, decided they should move the gold to a safe place on shore. They intended to hide it and retrieve it later.

Unknown to Marsh, most of the Sioux and Cheyenne were still on the Little Bighorn, but they were preparing to get out. They knew that the white man would be coming to avenge the deaths of the men killed in battle. They had won a huge victory, and in doing so, had ensured the destruction of their way of life. But Marsh didn't know that. He expected an attack at any moment.

They dragged the gold to shore and then headed toward Pine Ridge, little more than a charcoal shape in the blackness of the night. It was farther than Marsh thought and it took longer than he thought. But they eventually reached it, and began to search for a suitable place to stash their gold. One of the men found a small cave, hidden behind a pine tree partway up the steep slope.

Together, they hauled the gold into the cave, pushing it back as deep as they could. Outside again, they covered the entrance and then hurried back to the boat, still believing they would be killed before they could reach its safety.

The next morning, June 27th, Marsh turned around and found the right rendezvous. It was then that he learned what had happened on the Little Bighorn on June 25. The news was spreading, and the soldiers were retiring from the battlefield. Before there was time to do anything, the wounded from Reno's defense of the hilltop were being moved to the boat for transport to the fort.

In the days following the battle, the boat was filled with wounded soldiers. Straw had been spread on the decks for their comfort because there wasn't enough room below in the cabins. After the horror of the hilltop, no one complained. They were thankful to have survived the battle long enough to get to the boat.

The *Far West* headed back toward Fort Abraham Lincoln. Marsh had forgotten about the gold. Longworth, afraid that he would be killed by the Indians, was right. His remains, those of his guards, and the wagon were found about fifty miles from the place he'd found the riverboat. The gold was not with him, and there were many who believed that Indians wouldn't have stolen it. They figured the treasure had been hidden in the mountains close to where the bodies had been found. That was where treasure hunters began searching, once the story got out.

Because of the circumstances, Marsh assumed that Longworth had returned to Bozeman. He didn't know that Longworth had died. Marsh, and the two men with him, were the only people who knew what had happened.

There are no indications that any of them ever recovered the gold. They might have searched for it, but because they had hidden it at night, in unfamiliar terrain, while watching for Sioux or Cheyenne, it makes sense that they couldn't find the right location.

There are few other clues. According to the logbook, the captain and his two officers were missing only about three and a half hours. That means they couldn't have strayed too far from the boat. They were, after all, traveling at night, over rough ground, carrying a fairly heavy load. That would have slowed them considerably.

Unlike so many other treasure stories, there is some documentation to support this tale. The logbook of the *Far West* exists, as do the records showing Longworth had been entrusted with a shipment of gold. And there are no indications that anyone ever recovered any of it. As far as can be determined, the gold is still there, hidden in a shallow cave on the Pine Ridge, not that far from the river or the Little Bighorn battlefield.

PART V

APPENDIX

18

A DIRECTORY OF LOST TREASURES

—

UNITED STATES

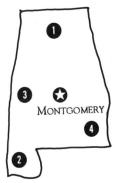

ALABAMA

❶ ATHENS

As the Civil War was ending, men loyal to the Southern cause collected a large amount of gold and silver coins. They sealed the treasure in two large crates. A man named Hansen, with two soldiers, wanted to take the money to Montgomery, but Union forces prevented it. Instead, they tried to find General Hood in Tennessee.

Near Athens, the wagon with the treasure got stuck in a bog. While the men worked to free it, a small Union patrol found them. Believing the wagon contained weapons and ammunition, the Union sergeant ordered the wagon unloaded. Hansen and his men shot it out with the Union patrol. Three of the Yankees were killed, as were Hansen's two friends. A wounded Union soldier escaped.

Hansen dumped the treasure in the bog to conceal it from the Union armies. He then made his way to the home of a friend and told him the story, giving him the general location of the treasure.

Hansen never had a chance to recover the gold and silver. He was killed by Union soldiers shortly afterward. His friend searched for the treasure unsuccessfully.

❷ MOBILE BAY

A pirate, known as Gasparilla, is said to have buried a number of treasure caches around the Mobile Bay area.

❸ MYRTLEWOOD

In 1860, a tax collector was stopped by bandits who wanted his strongbox filled with $30,000 in gold. The tax collector tossed the gold into the Tambigbee River, near a ford. The robbers killed the tax collector, but were unable to recover the gold. There is no record of it having been found by anyone.

❹ NEWTON

A band of guerrillas, under a Rebel colonel named Joseph Sanders, raided the town. The locals, apparently having some advance warning, were afraid of losing the town's treasury. Three men were selected to bury a box filled with gold coins. Sanders did attack and four men were killed, three of them being the men who had hidden the gold. There is no evidence that any map had been created, or that anyone else knew where the gold had been hidden.

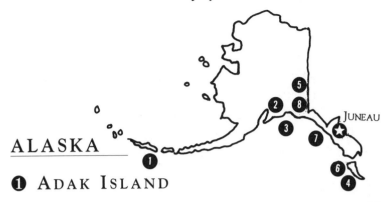

❶ ADAK ISLAND

Captain Gregory Dwargstof sold the skins of a very successful sealing operation. He supposedly buried about a million dollars on Red Bluff Hill on the island in 1892. Gold coins have been found on the hill, but the large cache has eluded treasure hunters.

❷ ANCHORAGE

Two prospectors, Olaf Swendson and Antonio Pauzza, found several ore-bearing ledges in the Talkeetna Mountains. The gold ore was so rich, they could chop it out with an ax. They carried out enough to retire for life and refused to ever return.

❸ CHITINA

A card shark and crooked dealer, Cortez D. Thompson, managed to accumulate about $50,000 through his card playing. He buried it to keep it out of the hands of others. A brawl with Soapy Smith forced Thompson to flee, apparently leaving his gold behind.

❹ DALL ISLAND

A Frenchman traded in a small general store at Howkan using gold to pay for his supplies. Although the storekeeper tried to convince the Frenchman to tell him where he got his gold, the Frenchman refused. Indians hired to track him always lost him before he led them to the gold.

Finally, in 1889, the Frenchman left the area never to return. His camp, however, was found a few years later on the north side of Dall Island.

❺ EAGLE

A cache of $50,000 was buried during the 1890s, somewhere between Eagle and Dawson, Canada.

❻ HARRIS RIVER

A man stole gold ore from one mine and hid it in another. There are supposed to be eighteen sacks of this ore hidden.

❼ TAKU ISLAND

A British ship, *Islander*, sank near Icy Point about nine miles from Juneau in 1901. Although carrying an estimated three million dollars in gold, nuggets, dust, and bullion, salvage operations have only recovered about a quarter of a million dollars.

❽ ST. ELIAS MOUNTAINS

Three prospectors near the Yukon River saw the sun reflecting from an island on a small lake. They crossed to the island and found it covered with nuggets. They built a cabin and spent the following weeks collecting the gold and hiding it in a nearby cave.

As so often happens in these sorts of stories, the local Indians attacked. One of the prospectors was killed, but the other two escaped, both eventually reaching the lower United States.

One of the survivors was badly injured in the escape. The other, more healthy, returned to Alaska the next summer, but disappeared. The gold should still be in the cave.

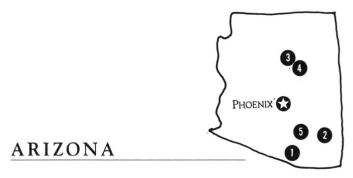

ARIZONA

❶ BABOQUIVARI MOUNTAINS

During the 1870s, a cavalry troop was chasing a band of Apaches, trying to intercept them before they escaped into Mexico. The cavalry stopped to water their horses at the base of a cliff where water was held in two "tanks," that is, small natural basins.

As the soldiers drank, they noticed gold nuggets at the bottom of the pools. Naturally, they were more interested in the gold than in chasing Apaches, but the officer in command overruled them. Surprisingly, the soldiers remounted, and headed off after the Indians.

Once the patrol was over and the men were back at the fort, several of them asked to be discharged. That was denied. Two decided they would desert. They stole two horses and supplies, and rode to the pools where the gold was. The water had dried up, but the gold was still there. They overloaded the horses and then made their way across the desert. When a patrol caught up, the horses were dead, gold was scattered across the desert, and one of the deserters had died. The survivor told of his ordeal before he, too, expired.

Other soldiers tried to find the gold but if they did, no one ever admitted it. The rich deposit is in the Baboquivari Mountains to the west of Arizona Route 286.

❷ DOS CABEZAS (GHOST TOWN)

Once again, we have Spanish gold and an Indian massacre. The story is that Mexicans controlled a wagon train filled with gold. Each night, the gold was unloaded and hidden for fear of thieves. One morning, before they could reclaim the treasure, the camp was attacked and everyone was killed except a small boy. He hid during the day and, with the help of local Mexicans, made his way back into Mexico.

When he grew up, he tried to find the treasure, which consisted of a gold, life-sized statue of the Virgin; a huge gold crucifix; and gold dust and nuggets. The only clue is that the site lies between two hills where the dry stream bed of the Willcox can be seen.

❸ FLAGSTAFF

Herman Wolf, a trader in the area in the late nineteenth century, is said to have buried the wealth he accumulated over thirty years. Small caches of gold or silver were found in 1901 and in 1966. The majority of the estimated quarter of a million dollars has not been found. Wolf's store was on the Little Colorado

River, northwest of Leupp, off the Santa Fe Trail near Canyon Diablo.

❹ Sycamore Canyon

George Mose Casner is said to have buried, or hidden, several small caches of gold southeast of Flagstaff. The legend is that he buried five Dutch ovens, each holding about $20,000 in gold coins. He also bored holes in trees, hid money in the holes, and then plugged them. Two small caches have been found.

❺ Wilcox

The Alvord gang stole about $60,000 in gold bullion and coin and is reported to have buried it along the trail between Cochise and Wilcox in the northern part of the state.

ARKANSAS

❶ Avants Mountain

John Avants told of a stranger who visited him sometime after the end of the Civil War. The stranger was searching for two springs close together. There, he said, would be a treasure lost by the Spanish. According to him, the Spaniards had been attacked by Indians. They knew that with the wagons of gold they had with them, they could never escape. They buried the gold, and the body of one of the men killed by the Indians.

The Spaniards escaped, and made their way back into Mexico where they told the story including the detail of the two springs. Avants said that he had thoroughly explored the area and knew of no place where there were two springs. The stranger searched, but couldn't find the landmarks.

Several years later, Avants's sons did find an area that matched the description. They also found some spikes driven into trees and some strange markings on them. Years after that, the boys told another relative about the stranger. The relative said that he knew of the place and had plowed up a human skull there. They all searched for the treasure, but never found it.

❷ Bee Creek

Strangely, during the Civil War, a small group of Indians were passing through Arkansas with gold and silver coins stolen during raids on Midwestern towns. The Indians suspected they were being followed by a large group of white men who would steal the money from them. They buried the treasure and burned their wagons on top of the spot. They planned to return to recover it and two of them did. However, they couldn't find the place where the treasure was hidden.

❸ Coweta Falls

There is a legend that Indians in the area buried a pot of gold in the walls of the bluff. The cave is marked by pictographs of a falls, a spring, an Indian moccasin, a snake, and a pot of gold.

❹ FAYETTEVILLE

William Flynn is said to have buried gold and silver worth more than $100,000. In addition, a family named Hermann buried five jars of gold coins during the Civil War. They eventually recovered three of them.

❺ MORRILTON

Edgar Mason is said to have buried about $60,000 in gold in a washtub near his cabin. Later, when he tried to find it, he failed. The site is about twenty miles east of Morrilton.

CALIFORNIA

❶ CALIFORNIA–ARIZONA BORDER

Earl Dorr, during the late 1890s, found an underground river that is believed to contain one of the richest, if not the richest, deposit of gold in the world. Dorr headed in to file a claim but discovered someone else had already filed one. Dorr returned to the natural opening and blasted it shut. Cavers (spelunkers) have since found the underground river and even the natural entrance and vault where Dorr had burned his name with his carbide lamp.

❷ GONZALES

Robbers stole over three quarters of a million dollars from Tom Sing in 1875. Rumors suggest they buried the safe on the banks of the Salinas River, halfway between Gonzales and Chualar, in a stand of pine a couple of hundred yards from the river. A posse killed the robbers before they learned that the safe had been hidden.

❸ MORENO

Bandits robbed the Bradshaw Route staff office in Beaumont, fleeing with about $20,000 in gold coins. The next morning, the robbers were ambushed by a sheriff's posse. The gold, however, was not on the bodies of the robbers, nor was it hidden in their camp. A search of the surrounding territory failed to turn up anything. The robbers must have buried their haul somewhere between where they stole it and where they were killed.

❹ NELSON POINT

Francis Lingard was looking for water in the High Sierras when he found a small stream that spilled into a lake. Scattered in the stream's channel and out into the lake were gold nuggets. It was obvious to Lingard that the gold had been carried into the lake from somewhere above.

Lingard gathered up as much of the gold as he could and began walking out of the area. Soon he realized that he had more gold than he could carry, so he stashed some of it at the base of a pine tree. He finally reached Nelson Point and bought a hundred dollars worth of supplies, paying for it with a gold nugget. He flashed other nuggets, showing those present that he had found quite a few.

Some time later, Lingard reappeared, bought more supplies and again paid with gold. When he came back a third time, he told store owner, John Carrington, that he was broke. He had no more gold. He told Carrington about the lake, but he had been unable to find it again.

Carrington staked him, but Lingard failed once more. Other parties were organized to search for the lake and the gold, but they never found it. Lingard, or someone, believed that high water had hidden the area. Rumors have it that Lingard was later shot, possibly by gold hunters who were angry that he couldn't find the lake of gold.

❺ PIEDRA RIVER

Near Chimney Rock are several sacks of gold nuggets and gold dust buried by Indians. They had attacked and killed a number of prospectors, stolen the gold, and hidden it.

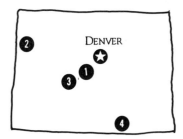

COLORADO

❶ HANDCART GULCH

The Reynolds gang robbed several different places, accumulating nearly $200,000 in gold and silver coins. They buried the treasure up the Hardcart Creek near the place where it joins the South Platte River. The gang was surprised and captured by a posse near the location but there is no evidence that the treasure was recovered.

❷ POOL CANYON

The Hanson brothers supposedly found a rich mine that they worked for a period of time. There is supposed to be twenty-five pounds of raw gold in the tunnel. The brothers were killed without revealing the location of the mine.

❸ SALINA

Three men working on a highway project, sometime in 1938 or 1939, had a few days off. They wandered the area, finding a mine shaft with old, rusting tools scattered around it. It looked as though the mine had been abandoned in a hurry. They searched but found nothing: no bleaching bones, no grave. Any mine that was worth anything would not have been abandoned.

The men, however, picked up some samples that looked as if they contained ore. The testing, for some reason, wasn't accomplished right away. The ore was rich in gold, but the men, who were off on another project, never returned to search for the mine.

❹ TRINIDAD

Train robbers made off with a quarter of a million dollars in gold coins. A sheriff's posse caught and killed the robbers but did not recover the gold.

Spaniards, exploring the areas of southern Colorado, discovered gold where they didn't expect it. They began preparing to mine and refine the gold, digging the tunnels and building the smelting equipment. Then, without explanation, they abandoned the site. They did what they could to hide the location, even covering their trail as they came down off the mountain.

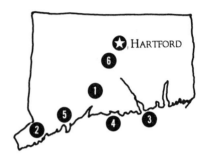

CONNECTICUT

❶ CLARKE'S ISLAND (IN THE CONNECTICUT RIVER)

Captain Kidd met with another pirate, Whisking Clarke, to bury two chests containing an estimated half a million in gold, jewels, and other valuables. This was just before he surrendered to authorities in Boston. With his wife, and his lawyer, James Emmot, he was sent to England for trial.

Although it has been suggested that Emmot persuaded Kidd that he would not be condemned, Kidd was tried by an English court and then executed. Emmot returned to recover the cache. He found the markers but no treasure.

Before he died, he told others the secret. The real problem is that the river has changed course a number of times and the forest has grown down to the shoreline.

❷ NORWALK

The "treasure" is the result of a documented train wreck on May 9, 1853. Thaddeus Birke, an Englishman who had taken up residence in New York City as a jeweler, was on the train. He carried with him, in two leather-covered, hardwood trunks, some $50,000 in jewelry, including gold bracelets, earrings, and rings holding diamonds, emeralds, and rubies.

When he boarded the train, Birke set the two trunks on the seat opposite him where he could watch them. When the train ran through the red signals and plunged into the river, Birke was killed and the trunks lost.

Rescue and later salvage operations failed to recover the smaller bits of luggage. Birke's trunks containing the jewels have never been reported as recovered.

❸ OLD LYME

Captain Kidd is said to have buried some sort of treaure under a large boulder.

❹ STONY BROOK

Sometimes called Money Island. Local legends suggest that some kind of treasure is buried on Trimble Island.

❺ STRATFORD POINT

Fishermen reported they saw Captain Kidd burying an ironbound wooden chest deep in the sand.

⑥ WETHERSFIELD

Captain Kidd sailed up the Connecticut River to a spot once called Tyron's Landing. There he buried a wooden chest that contained jewels.

DELAWARE

❶ BLACKBIRD CREEK

It is believed that Blackbeard buried a chest of treasure on the banks of the creek.

❷ BOMBAY HOOK ISLAND

Captain Kidd is reported to have hidden nearly a million dollars in gold, silver plate, and ingots on the island.

❸ KELLY ISLAND

Seaman James Gillian helped Captain Kidd bury a treasure of an estimated $300,000 in gold and silver. It was hidden between two bare trees and a large rock. After Kidd was executed, Gillian was going to return to recover the treasure, but never did.

❹ PURGATORY WOODS

In an area that is marked by White Clay Creek and St. George's Creek, between Newark and Cooch's Bridge, a large wooden bowl filled with gold coins and sprinkled with a few made of silver, was buried. Thomas Cooch buried the treasure in 1777, to keep it out of the hands of the British when they took over his mill before burning it.

❺ RELIANCE

Fat Patty Cannon and two partners, who ran a tavern on the Maryland–Delaware border, murdered and robbed slave dealers and buyers. When they were finally caught, thirty-seven bodies were found buried near the tavern. Fat Patty killed herself to avoid trial, having already killed one of her partners. It is alleged that she and her partners buried between $75,000 and $150,000 in gold coins during her murderous rampage. Local farmers have reported finding small caches of coins that total about $12,000.

❻ WEDGE

This is an area claimed by Pennsylvania, Delaware, and Maryland. Because of the claims by different states, there has been a lack of law enforcement in the region. There are rumors that all sorts of criminals used the area and buried various types of loot in it from about 1893 through 1921.

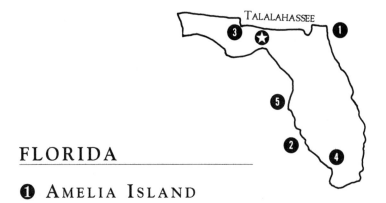

FLORIDA

❶ AMELIA ISLAND

The island, near the Georgia border, was reported to be a pirate meeting place. Gold coins have been found, and local rumors claim that almost $200,000 has been recovered. The locals claim that more treasure is still hidden.

❷ CHARLOTTE HARBOR

The Calusa Indians managed to recover some gold and silver from wrecked Spanish ships, which they used to trade for supplies. The tribe was wiped out by the Spanish, and the sites of their treasure never found.

❸ CHATTAHOOCHIE RIVER

The Seminoles buried a huge treasure of American and British coins during the war fought with Andrew Jackson in the 1830s. The best information is that the it's buried in swamp silt on the extreme edge of the Florida–Georgia border, in Jackson County.

❹ EVERGLADES

In the 1920s, the Ashley gang robbed a number of banks. The estimated take was about $150,000 in currency. There was never any report that the cash has been recovered. It's believed that they had an island in the Everglades where they stashed the loot.

❺ HONEYMOON ISLAND

No real stories of treasure or gold, but after storms, coins wash up on shore. There are many such areas along the Atlantic Coast where storms leave riches in their wake. Some kind of a treasure ship or chest is in the waters near the island.

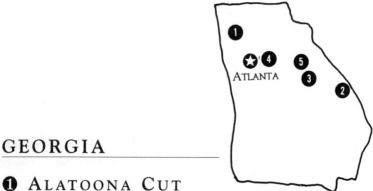

GEORGIA

❶ ALATOONA CUT

Indians supposedly worked a gold mine on the C.M. Jones farm on Pumpkinsville Creek. There might be gold bars or treasure buried in the mine.

❷ COFITACHEQUI

As de Soto made his way through the area, he demanded treasure from the local Indians. They showed him pearls they had gathered. Since the Indians used fire to open the oysters, the pearls weren't fine, but de Soto took 350 pounds of them and later buried them somewhere along his route through Georgia.

❸ LITTLE RIVER

Jeremiah Griffin set up Georgia's first stamp mill and supposedly took out $80,000 in gold bullion. He died in 1847, after hiding more than $100,000 in gold somewhere along the Little River in Wilkes County.

❹ STONE MOUNTAIN

The Spanish, taking treasure from the Aztecs, for some reason were traveling through what is now Georgia. They were attacked by Indians and killed. The Indians took what they could use and buried the gold at the site of the massacre.

❺ WASHINGTON

The last meeting of the Confederate Congress took place in Washington. It was rumored that Jefferson Davis and the rest of his cabinet buried Confederate gold on the lot now occupied by the Wilkes County Courthouse.

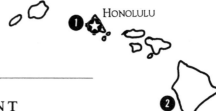

HAWAII

❶ KAENA POINT

Pirates are reported to have buried six treasure-filled chests at Kaena Point on Oahu in 1823, near a wall made of fitted stones at the top of a hill.

❷ KEALAKEKUA

Pirates buried a number of chests and boxes filled with gold and silver and jewels in 1818. This treasure is rumored to be worth several million dollars and was hidden by a pirate named Turner.

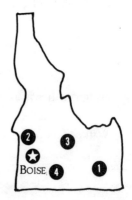

IDAHO

❶ BLACKFOOT

A bandit held up a stage and made off with 250 pounds in gold bullion. He hid the gold in a cave among the lava beds near the stage road, but he was killed before he could recover it.

❷ IDAHO COUNTY

Miners worked a place called Dry Diggins Ridge in the south-western part of the county. When they were attacked by Indians, they buried their gold in a blue bucket and then tried to escape. None of them returned to claim the treasure. One of the men told the story to his son before he died. The son returned many times but never found anything.

❸ ROOT HOG DIVIDE

Gold was regularly shipped from the mines in Custer County. A bandit held up one of the shipments and took the gold. Later he was found gambling with about $5,000 on him. He agreed to take law enforcement officers to the rest of the loot, but escaped at the first opportunity.

Later a man from New Mexico appeared with a map showing the location of a cave in the lava beds. He said the bandit had given him the map to recover the gold because he was afraid to return to Idaho. The man found nothing and returned to New Mexico empty-handed.

❹ SHOSHONE ICE FIELD

Two robbers preyed on the miners in the Boise Basin. Trying to escape with their loot, they were caught by a posse near the ice fields. They took to the lava beds on foot but were eventually caught and then killed. The estimated $75,000 they had stolen was nowhere near the bodies. It was assumed that it was hidden somewhere between the point where their horses were killed and where they were caught.

ILLINOIS

❶ BENNINGTON

An Indian appeared in 1907 with a crude map, explaining that members of his tribe had buried three kegs of gold coins when they were forced from the area by white men. The cache was located only three or four feet from the surface along a small stream called Sugar Creek.

A farmer assisted the Indian who referred to his map several times. The Indian seemed to find the landmarks he needed and he did dig, but he found no kegs of gold. Disappointed, the Indian left the area never to return. There is no indication that the three kegs of gold were ever found.

❷ CENTRALIA

James Gregory operated the only general supply store in the area for many years. His was a cash-only business; he didn't like banks. He kept his money hidden somewhere on his property. He died suddenly of a stroke in 1925, and his wife searched for the money but never found it. As far as anyone knows, the cache is still hidden in one of his pastures.

❸ KASKASKIA

The French ordered the construction of a fort along the Mississippi, which is now a historic site south of St. Louis, near Chester, IL. The French engineer, Sebastian Vauhan, used locals for the labor and didn't bother to pay them, though the French crown had provided gold for the purpose. Vauhan was ordered back to France. Knowing he would be executed for stealing the gold, he committed suicide. The gold has not been found and may be buried somewhere on the historic site. Treasure hunting on historic sites is forbidden by law.

❹ NAUVOO

The Mormons, before they began their trek to Utah, buried the church treasure under one of the buildings. Forced from the town by those who hated them, it is rumored that the Mormons were unable to recover the gold. They made plans to return, but there is no mention that it ever happened. The gold is still probably buried under one of the old buildings or building sites in the area.

❺ STRAVED ROCK

A cache of $100,000 in gold coins was buried somewhere near Straved Rock on the Illinois River by a Frenchman named Tonty.

❻ WALKERVILLE TOWNSHIP

The richest man in the county, Azariah Sweetin, didn't trust banks. He made his money during the Civil War, selling beef to the government. He was paid in gold coins, which he buried on his farm known as the Hartwell Ranch.

Sometime after the war, while out riding, Sweetin fell from his horse. Although he recovered, his memory was impaired. He couldn't remember where he buried his money. The cache of gold coins has not been recovered.

INDIANA

❶ SILVER CREEK

Sometime about 1775, Indians stole a keg of silver coins during a raid. They buried the treasure about five miles from the mouth of what is now called Silver Creek. Many have searched for the silver, but no one has found it.

A New York merchant camped on the creek and was known to have a large quantity of silver coins with him. He started on a trading trip but never returned to his home. It is believed that he buried his silver somewhere on the creek before he left.

❷ TREMONT

Raiders stole gold and furs in Michigan, and escaped to the South. They were caught, with the French recovering the furs, but had apparently buried the gold near Tremont. An official report claimed the furs were found, but they learned nothing about the gold.

❸ YORK

This is another story of a merchant who didn't trust banks. George Downing accumulated a fortune through farming and cattle raising. Downing's brother also buried money on the farm. Two local men tortured Downing, trying to get him to reveal the location of the estimated $100,000 in gold coins. Downing died without telling anyone where the money was hidden.

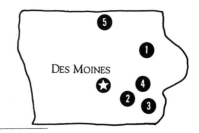

IOWA

❶ CEDAR COUNTY

The Ives brothers, like so many others, buried their wealth rather than put it into a local bank. Relatives did find about $200,000 in large-sized currency. Those same relatives knew that the Ives brothers had a stash of the "new" smaller-sized currency as well but no one has ever located that.

❷ EDDYVILLE

The postmaster at Eddyville received a letter from a man who identified himself only as "Le Barge." He claimed that he, with two companions, had struck it rich in the gold fields of the Black Hills. Each had a gallon jug filled with gold dust and nuggets. On their way home, they camped near Eddyville where they got into a poker game with one of the men, William Gunton, who won most of the gold. Le Barge accused him of cheating and in the fight that followed, Gunton was killed. Le Barge and his friend cut off Gunton's head, burned it, and then buried the body elsewhere; they were afraid they would be accused of killing Gunton for his share. Using the grave as the center point, they buried the three jugs in three different locations.

A search inspired by the letter failed to find the treasure. Twenty years later, a road crew found a skull that had been burned. It set off another round of treasure hunting, but to date no one has found any of the gold.

❸ FAIRFIELD

Three Indians buried gold given to them as part of a treaty settlement. Later the Indians were killed in a tribal war and the gold was not recovered. It is believed that it's buried near the "Bonnifield" cabin in Jefferson County.

❹ FORT MCKAY

Zachary Taylor received about $30,000 in gold to pay his soldiers. Worried about the Indians, the gold was buried, but in the battle that followed, the men who knew the location were killed. Taylor searched for the money for several days, but never found it. There is no evidence that anyone has ever located the treasure.

❺ MASON CITY

Thomas Nelson, a ranch hand, soldier of fortune, and prospector worked on the Wheeler Ranch in Cerro Gordo County in the 1880s. He was seen counting tall stacks of gold coins. Afraid that someone would steal the gold, he buried it along the Winnebago

River somewhere between the Wheeler Ranch and a horseshoe bend. He was sure that he could find the gold again when he wanted it.

That apparently was not the case because he was seen walking the banks of the river searching for years after. He left the area once, to go to Alaska, but returned to search again. Eventually he gave up, telling the locals that whoever found the gold could have it.

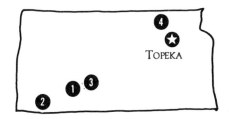

KANSAS

❶ DODGE CITY

This is another tale of an Indian massacre with a single survivor. A group of Mexicans were traveling from Santa Fe to Missouri when they were attacked. They drove off the Indians but a seige began. Over the next five days the Indians killed the remainder of the defenders. They then burned the wagons and left. The one man who survived crept back into the area and buried the silver among the ruined wagons. There are supposed to be forty-two bags containing one thousand silver coins each buried four miles west of Dodge City.

❷ LIBERAL

The Morgan brothers, like so many others, saved everything they made, did not spend a dime they didn't have to, and buried their wealth on their farm. The brothers were murdered and their house burned to the ground to hide the crime. No one ever found any money on their property, though hundreds have searched for it.

❸ OFFERLE

Once again, Indians are responsible. Prospectors returning from the California gold fields camped near Offerle. They buried $50,000 in gold coins along a creek. They were attacked the next morning and all were killed but an eight-year-old girl. Years later she returned to the site to search for the gold but never found it.

❹ SENECA

Two prospectors returning from California buried about $85,000 in gold on the South Fork of the Nemaha River before going into town. There, they somehow became involved in a brawl. One was killed and the other fled never to return. His sons, however, did make a search many years later but they were unable to locate the gold.

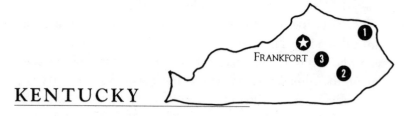

KENTUCKY

❶ GREENUP

A sudden, strong storm chased two hunters into a cave along what is now thought to be Raccoon Creek. While waiting for the storm to end, they explored and found gold and silver ore and many old Indian artifacts. When the storm finally ended, they both headed for their homes, but it was still dark and rainy. They were never able to find the cave again.

❷ LEVI JACKSON WILDERNESS ROAD STATE PARK

A group of pioneers were camped in the area when they were attacked by Indians. They had elected one man as treasurer and when the attack began, he hid the treasure consisting of gold, silver, and jewels. Twenty-six of the settlers were killed, including the treasurer. Searches of the area failed to produce any clues.

❸ LEXINGTON

John Campbell bought land and then built a cabin at Allegan Hall. The cabin and land were later sold to William Pettit who eventually became wealthy. He converted everything he could into gold, frightened by the coming of the Civil War. He buried the gold coins but died before he recovered them.

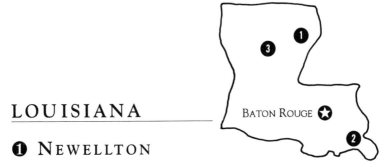

LOUISIANA

❶ NEWELLTON

Civil War Confederate Colonel Norman Frisbee buried his family fortune, rumored to be one million dollars, in the marshland near the ruins of his plantation. There is no indication that Frisbee ever recovered the treasure made up of gold and silver coins, a huge silver bell, and other valuables.

❷ PHOENIX

The French built a fort that could be reached only by boat. They later abandoned it when the settlement at New Orleans began to grow. It's rumored that the French buried $150,000 in gold on the site of the old fort. Gold coins have begun to surface, suggesting that high water in the area has disturbed the treasure.

❸ WINNFIELD

A Spanish treasure caravan was working its way through the area. When they ran into Indians, the Spanish attacked, killing all but three. The survivors found reinforcements. The Spanish decided to divide into two parties to work their way to Natchez, Mississippi. Their problem was that several of their mules had been killed. They couldn't take all their treasure with them and were forced to bury part of it in man-made caves. None of that treasure has never been recovered.

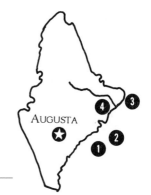

MAINE

❶ DEER ISLAND IN CASCO BAY

Treasure hunters and diggers have found various bits of gold and gold coins, some minted in 1609, have been recovered. A treasure estimated at three and a half million dollars was buried somewhere on the island. There are stories that one chest has been found.

❷ EDGECOMB

A small treasure, estimated at half a million, was buried by Sam Trask, a trusted seaman of Captain Kidd.

❸ FORT POINT COVE

Four chests stolen from a ship in the Indian Ocean are rumored to have been buried by Captain Kidd. The estimated value is about a million and a half.

❹ MACHIAS RIVER

Two pirates, Bellamy and Williams, constructed a fortification with underground chambers, the exact location now lost. They hid their considerable treasure, now estimated at several million dollars, on this site. The two pirate leaders and several of the crew were killed when their ship broke up in a storm. The remainder were captured and hanged and the buried treasure was never recovered.

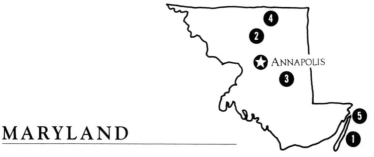

MARYLAND

❶ ASSATEAGUE ISLAND

The *Indies Ballard*, a triple-masted sloop, sank near the island in 1792. She carried $130,000 in gold and two searches have failed to produce any of the treasure.

❷ BALTIMORE

About $70,000 was hidden at the Mansion House. The treasure was either concealed in the house or on the ground near it.

❸ EASTON

State Senator, William Perry, buried the family riches each year before he went to the state legislature. In 1799, after having buried the yearly treasure, he died of a heart attack in Annapolis. A servant who helped him was killed in a buggy accident before he could share the secret. The treasure is still somewhere on the plantation.

❹ UNION MILLS

A German immigrant, Ahrwud, who worked as a silversmith, was shown a silver mine on Rattlesnake Hill. Ahrwud worked the mine for about ten years and then told someone else about it. The Indians retaliated, killing Ahrwud and his daughter. They then hid the entrance to the mine to prevent anyone else from working it.

❺ WOODY KNOLL

According to a letter that the pirate Charles Wilson sent to his brother, nearly a million dollars in gold, silver, and jewels are buried in Worchester County. The letter said, "There are three creeks lying one hundred paces or more north of a second inlet about Chincoteague Island, which is at the southward end of the peninsula. At the head of the third creek to the northward is a bluff facing the Atlantic Ocean with three cedar trees growing on it, each about one and a third yards apart. Between these trees I buried ten chests, bars of silver, gold, diamonds and jewels. . . ."

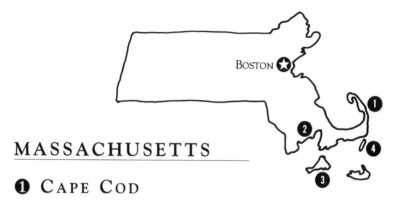

MASSACHUSETTS

❶ CAPE COD

Arthur Doane, a long-time resident of the area, saw pirates burying chests in 1831. As soon as the pirates were gone, Doane dug up the treasure and moved it. For nearly fifty years afterward he sold a few gold coins at a time to a friend. When he became ill, he told his friend where the chests were buried, but the friend could never find them.

❷ HOG ISLAND

John Breed, an Englishman, settled on Hog Island in Boston Bay. He hired an Indian to guard the entrance to a cave on the island. When he died, relatives searched the cave and found $5,000 hidden inside. They believed that more treasure was hidden somewhere but failed to find it.

❸ MARTHA'S VINEYARD

During the Revolutionary War, an elderly woman living alone buried her wealth when the British arrived. The woman survived, but could not remember exactly where she had hidden her treasure.

❹ MONOMOY ISLAND

Beach pirates, using false lights and buoys, lured ships close to shore where they were wrecked. The pirates would then steal everything they could carry away. Though no large treasure is rumored to be buried on the island, a search of the land and shallows nearby could yield a large number of gold or silver coins.

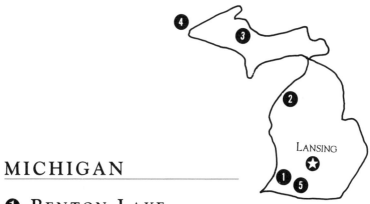

MICHIGAN

❶ BENTON LAKE

In 1874 a gang of bandits stole $74,000 in gold meant as a payroll for a logging camp. Afraid that the loggers would soon be after them, the bandits buried the gold. They put it in a large cast-iron stove, dug a deep hole, and covered it up.

❷ BENZIE COUNTY

The Chippewas decided to attack their enemies in Wisconsin. Before they began their expedition, the chief took all the gold they had, in two large copper kettles, and buried it. As the Chippewas approached the site of Green Bay, a storm swamped their canoes and many of the warriors, including the chief, were drowned.

❸ ESCANABA

The story is that a ship sank in the area carrying about four and a half million dollars in gold. This might have been sent from England with plans to get the treasure to the Confederacy. The ship was attacked and the guards are reported to have chained the chests together and dumped them into the shallow water with plans to recover the treasure later. There are no reports that the gold was ever recovered.

❹ HERMIT ISLAND

The real hermit of the island, Frederick Prentice, who had stone quarries on three of the islands, lived alone in his big house. When she saw the location, his bride refused to live there. Prentice lived out his life on Hermit Island, and when he died his fortune, estimated at several hundred thousand dollars, could not be located.

❺ PORT SHELDON

Nicholas Biddle, a banker, had visions of planned cities on the good harbors in Michigan. One of these, Port Sheldon in Ottawa County, was actually started, but the financing eventually collapsed. Biddle heard that some of his investors were planning to raid the town. Biddle hid about a quarter of a million in a well near the hotel he had built. The raid didn't happen, but Biddle was afraid to return for the money.

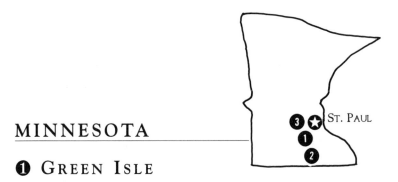

MINNESOTA

❶ GREEN ISLE

Two brothers buried $40,000 in gold and silver in Sibley County.

❷ HENDERSON

A small treasure of $10,000 in gold coins is hidden in a grove of trees.

Charles Ney owned and operated a brewery for many years in the town. When he died, the money he made could not be located and it was believed that he had hidden his wealth at the brewery. In 1926, a shaft was dug on the site of the brewery in search of the treasure vault but nothing was found.

❸ MINNEAPOLIS

During the Civil War, a man buried a large treasure, consisting mainly of gold, on the site of what is now the Old Soldier's Home. The man told a friend about the treasure before he died, but the friend couldn't find it. The property now belongs to the state.

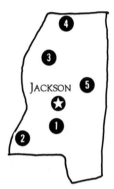

MISSISSIPPI

❶ BOGUE CHITTO RIVER

The Choctaws buried a government payment in gold for land at
the foot of the first hill north of the river in Lincoln County.

❷ DEVIL'S PUNCHBOWL

In an area that might be the remnant of an ancient meteorite strike,
several bandits and pirates have hidden treasure. Some of the caches
have probably been recovered, but there are others that remain.

❸ DODDSVILLE

A merchant who traveled the region hid seven fruit jars filled with
gold and silver coins in the woods near the town. He apparently
used alcohol in an attempt to keep the coins from corrosion.

❹ HOLLY SPRING

A Union paymaster buried $8,000 in gold in sight of the railroad
station to keep the Rebels from capturing it. He died before he
had a chance to recover it or reveal its location.

❺ LITTLE ROCK

Zackary Goforth accumulated his second fortune after the stock market crash in 1929. No longer trusting banks, Goforth buried his treasure in fruit jars. When he became sick, he tried to tell family members where he had hidden the money but failed. It is estimated that $7,000 in gold is still hidden in the area.

MISSOURI

❶ ADRIAN

A band of guerrillas, loosely affiliated with the South, robbed the town of Adrian during the Civil War. They were chased by Union troops, but stopped long enough to bury three bags of gold coins, worth about $90,000, near a tree. Before they could escape, they were caught in Kansas and all were killed in the battle. A wounded man told of burying the treasure before he died. He was unable to tell his captors exactly where it had been hidden.

❷ GALENA

The original silver mine was worked by the Spanish. They created crude silver bars but, before they could make use of their wealth, started fighting among themselves. The lone survivor, Pedro Diego, then hooked up with two Irishmen named Higgins and McCabe. Diego disappeared and not long afterward, the

Irishmen arrived in Boston boasting of their wealth hidden in Missouri. They didn't return, but a relative of Higgins sold the details of the mine to a man named Watson Johnson. Johnson is supposed to have found the mine and was found dead at the entrance. The silver bars are hidden in a cave about a mile or so from the mine.

❸ OZARK SPRINGS

During the Civil War, a group of men buried $35,000 in gold and silver in a long trench in front of an animal den on the northern end of a sinkhole. The men were caught by Rebel soldiers and all were shot with the exception of a Union deserter. He told relatives about the treasure as he lay dying in 1911.

❹ ST. LOUIS

Bonnie Heady and Carl Hall kidnapped little Bobby Greenlease. They obtained $600,000 in ransom. When they were captured, only $300,000 of the money was recovered. The remainder is reported to have been buried in two garbage cans along the Meremac River.

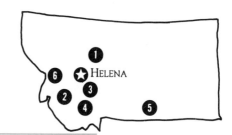

MONTANA

❶ CHINEE GRADE

While working on the railroad, Chinese workers collected a quantity of gold, which they kept in a five-pound baking tin. When the Chinese crew was ordered to pack to leave, they buried the tin, planning to come back for it later. They never did. The tin was buried at the foot of the Chinee Grade.

❷ DILLON

A hermit named Joseph K. Knoles made a fortune working the gold fields of Montana. He lived alone near Dillon. In 1872, he wrote to his sister, daughter, and son-in-law, telling them to come to visit him. He knew that he wouldn't live much longer and wanted to tell them where he had hidden his fortune in gold. His relatives didn't arrive in time. Knoles was dead by the time they got there. They searched the cabin and the grounds but found nothing. Knoles's fortune is still hidden somewhere around Dillon.

❸ GILMAN

A prospector named Oldendorf worked in the mountains to the west. In 1886, he shipped half a ton of pure gold from Great Falls and another half ton from Gilman. Instead of waiting for his payment, he told several men that he was returning to the mountains but would come back for his mail. He disappeared. No one ever found the gold mine that he was working.

❹ HIGHLAND CITY

The ghost town was once larger than Butte. One of the prospectors called Beastly Butler worked his claim alone. He filled the cans his food came in with gold and then buried the cans. He said that once his claim played out, he would recover his gold and go east. Butler was killed in a cave-in. Once he was buried, others searched for his treasure, but no one ever found anything.

❺ LITTLE BIG HORN

Two Cheyenne reported that after the battle with Custer's troops, they collected a large amount of paper money, stuffed it into a saddle bag, and hid it in the fork of a tree. It is known that the Seventh Cavalry wasn't paid until after they left Fort Abraham Lincoln so they wouldn't be tempted to desert. Much of the money was destroyed by warriors who didn't know what it was. However, some of them knew the value of the green paper.

❻ RAINY LAKE

The Henry Plummer gang buried $100,000 on the shore of the Rainy Lake in 1864.

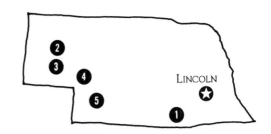

NEBRASKA

❶ ALEXANDRIA

While traveling, two ranchers from the area were attacked by Indians. They sought refuge in a cave, but the Indians captured and killed them. Their gold was not found with them and it is believed it was hidden in another, nearby cave. In 1908, a bag containing over fifty gold coins was discovered in the area, but the rest of the treasure remains.

❷ ALLIANCE

A team carrying freight stopped in an area known as Point of Rocks. One of the three men stole the gold, buried it nearby, and then returned to the camp. The crime wasn't discovered then and all three men continued to their final destination. There, it was learned the gold was missing and a fight broke out. The thief was killed in the fight but the gold was never found.

❸ DALTON

Sioux Indians attacked the stage station at Mud Springs. The stationmaster buried the gold stored there so that it would not fall into the hands of the Sioux. The men were able to defend themselves until help from nearby Army patrols came to the rescue. During the fight, the stationmaster was killed. No one knew where he had hidden the gold.

❹ PLATTE RIVER

A farmer named Anderson found about $100,000 in gold coins while plowing his farm. This was supposed to have been part of a Mormon treasure. Anderson, like many others, didn't like banks, so he reburied the treasure on one of the many islands in the Platte River near the Wood River and died without telling anyone exactly where the gold was hidden.

❺ RED WILLOW CREEK

An Army surveying party, carrying $3,000 in gold, spotted and attacked a small band of Indians. Before beginning the assault, they had buried their gold. More Indians, having heard the sound of firing, appeared and chased the surveyors from the original location into a stand of trees on Beaver Creek. The surveyors were all killed.

The Army found the remains of the surveyors some time later. They searched for the gold and the wagons, but found nothing.

NEVADA

❶ BODIE

Milton Sharp stole a number of large gold bars from a Wells Fargo stage. He hid the gold near the old Bodie to Carson road between Wellington and Walley's. Everything was recovered with the exception of a single, eight pound bar of gold. There is no evidence that he ever found the missing bar.

❷ CARSON CITY

Big Jack Davis hid just over $20,000 in an outhouse in Carson City. Shortly after that, Davis was arrested for his part in a train robbery. Paroled for helping stop a prison break, he was killed in 1877 by a Wells Fargo guard as he tried to rob a stagecoach. He never did recover the gold he hid.

❸ DELAMAR

An official at the Jackrabbit Mine stole some $70,000 with the help of an assayer. He buried the gold but died before he could recover it. The assayer had no idea where the treasure was buried.

❹ Pyramid Lake

Chinese laborers would enter abandoned gold mines, taking out small amounts of gold that was left. They accumulated enough to fill two chests. They were attacked by Indians and killed. The chests were left at the base of a cliff near the lake.

❺ Reno

Allen Bruce stole $34,000 in currency from a government payroll in California. He eventually buried some of it near the River Inn. All but $12,000 has been accounted for. Bruce said that he carefully wrapped the money in sections of inner tube to protect them. There is no evidence that either Allen or his accomplice, James Smith, recovered the missing $12,000.

❻ Searchlight

A prospector, camping one night near Searchlight, discovered that someone else had used the campsite before him. He found a buried skillet that contained very rich gold ore. The prospector also found the vein that had been covered by the first man. He tried to mark the location and then went to file his claim but when he returned, he found nothing.

❼ Silver City

A dying miner reported that three bars of gold had been hidden in the ruined basement of an old hotel near the Devil's Gate. There has never been any report that anyone found the gold.

❽ TREASURE CITY

A miner decided that he wanted to settle an argument with a bartender in Shermantown. Although there was a snowstorm raging and he was advised not to go, he made the trip anyway. He eventually arrived at the bar, but before he died, he mumbled things about a "flat rock" and "steep trail." Although people knew he had about $3,200 in gold coins, when he arrived he had only ten dollars. Apparently he hid the rest somewhere between Treasure City and Shermantown.

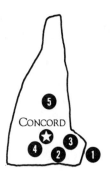

NEW HAMPSHIRE

❶ BOON ISLAND

A British ship, the *Nottingham*, sank near Boon Island just off the Isles of Shoals in 1710. In the ship's safe were rubies then reported to be worth over a million dollars.

❷ CROMWELL FALLS

A fur trader, John Cromwell, built his post in the area of the Merrimack River. The Indians believed that he was cheating them and made plans to burn his trading post. Cromwell learned of it, buried his treasure, and fled, returning to England where he died in 1661.

❸ DURHAM

The British governor, John Wentworth, fleeing advocates of a break with the British Empire, took seven chests filled with treasure. He hoped to reach Canada and return once the revolution was suppressed. Along the way, he realized that the chests were slowing his escape, so he buried them. One was filled with gold coins and the others contained silverware and other valuables.

❹ LOTTERY BRIDGE

Counterfeiters operated in the area of the bridge in the 1840s. The bogus plates, which would be of little value, and a cache of good (meaning legal) coins are still hidden in a small cave near the bridge.

❺ WHITE HILLS

During the French and Indian War, Richard Rogers and his rangers attacked an Indian village called St. Francis. At the end of the battle, a group of the rangers raided the church, stealing gold candlesticks, a chalice, and a silver madonna.

During the escape, the rangers were separated from the main group. Chased by the French and Indians the stragglers were picked off quickly. Four men, carrying the statue of the Virgin, fled into the Great Notch area of the White Mountains. They were close to the Isreal River when one of the four grabbed the statue and threw it over a cliff. He hoped to escape and return to retrieve it later.

The four didn't survive, but the story of the statue did. Years later the remains of the party were found, but the silver statue was not.

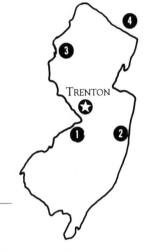

NEW JERSEY

❶ BURLINGTON

With all the discussion of Captain Kidd's caches along the eastern seaboard, it is nice to find the story of another pirate treasure. Blackbeard is said to have buried a treasure on a lot in Burlington, which the local historical society claims is the Florence Stewart lot. Although treasure hunters have searched, there are no reports that anyone has found anything.

❷ CLIFFORD BEACH

Kidd is reported to have buried a large cache along the beach. Some researchers claim that this has been documented. However, due to shoreline erosion, most treasure hunters now believe the loot is underwater.

❸ HARKERS HOLLOW

Patrick Flynn, known as the Hermit of Harkers Hollow, distrusted banks all his life. He hid his money, burying some of it on his property. When he died in 1903, the neighbors searched his land, finding about $3,000 in various locations.

When Flynn's sister was informed of his death, she traveled to New Jersey. She told the neighbors that the little bit of money they had found was only a small portion of his accumulated wealth.

❹ STORY'S FLAT (STATEN SOUND)

Here is another well-documented treasure complete with a fairly precise location. In 1905, the Mallory Shipping Line, which had brought nearly 7,700 silver pigs, each weighing about 100 pounds, loaded them on a barge to be taken to the American Smelting and Refining Company.

Sometime during the night, the load shifted, and the majority of the silver slipped overboard. It seems difficult to believe that tons of silver could fall into Staten Sound without the crew being aware of it, but the problem was not discovered until the next morning. Only about 200 of the ingots were left scattered on the deck.

A salvage company was hired and, using a combination of divers, steam shovels, and other activities, recovered the majority of the silver. Threats from local pirates, however, caused a suspension of the operations. All but 1,800 of the missing silver ingots were recovered. There is no indication that anyone has ever recovered the rest of the silver, though the records show that it remains on Story's Flat in Staten Sound off Sewaren.

NEW MEXICO

❶ ALBUQUERQUE

The Isleta Pueblo, which is south of Albuqerque, was rumored to have had a rich gold mine when the Spanish still controlled the area. Raids by the Apaches made it difficult for the priest to force the Indians to work the mine. Finally the Apaches captured the priest and killed him. They then erased all traces of the mine so that other white men would not find it.

❷ CABALLO MOUNTAINS

Pedro Navarez confessed to a priest, just before his execution in 1850, that he had hidden a huge treasure of silver in a cave. The spot is marked by a cross carved into a large rock.

❸ GRANTS

A plane carrying $100,000 for Alf Landon's political campaign crashed into the lava flow (the malpais) to the west and south of Albuquerque. The money has never been recovered.

❹ MOUNTAINAIR

A Spanish priest is reported to have hidden more than two mule loads of gold and silver on two small hills overlooking the old mission site near Gran Quivara National Monument. The treasure is rumored to be worth more than $120 million.

❺ RIO BONITO

In south central Lincoln County is a cave filled with silver bars. The treasure was hidden by Indians who had taken it from the Spanish. A man identified only as Hawkins found the silver, took some of it out, and then concealed the entrance. He sold the silver in Albuquerque but when he returned, couldn't find the cave.

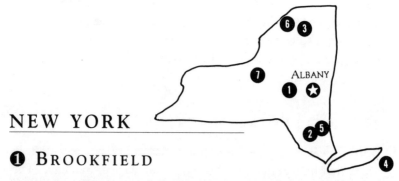

NEW YORK

❶ BROOKFIELD

The Loomis gang hid $40,000 or more in gold and silver at their camp in Nine Mile Swamp. Although many have searched for it, no one has reported finding it.

❷ GOSHEN

During the American Revolution, Claudius Smith remained loyal to the British. The war provided him with an excuse to kill and rob and he, his sons, and his gang, attacked those friendly to the American cause. All members of the gang were eventually captured and hanged, or killed in fights with American authorities.

In the early nineteenth century, Smith's grandchildren appeared in the area with a map. All they recovered was a cache of rusty weapons. Twenty years later another group with another map arrived, but they failed to find anything. The treasure is said to be buried in the hills around Goshen or in caves near Tuxedo in Orange County.

❸ FOLLENSBY'S POND

Moses Follensby, a man of noble English birth, lived his life quietly near the small lake that now bears his name. When he died, his private papers and journals suggested that he had hidden about $400,000 in the area near his cabin.

❹ MONTAUK POINT

The pirate Joe Bradish buried $300,000 in gold and jewels in several boxes at the extreme eastern end of the island.

❺ PAWLING

A bag of gold and silver, stolen during the Revolutionary War, was buried in a meadow near Pawling. It was left by a British officer before he was hanged until dead.

❻ ST. LAWRENCE RIVER

In 1760, as the French were being driven from the area, Marquis de Lewis buried a large cache of gold. Years later, a man, supposedly the grandson of de Lewis, found 400 pounds of gold that had been fused together when the fort was burned. He and a companion broke the mass apart but could only carry away some of it.

When a storm threatened the boat, the man tied several bags of gold around his waist. The boat sank, the man drowned, and his companion couldn't save him. Some of the gold remains on the island, and the rest is at the bottom of the river.

❼ SULPHUR SPRINGS

A traveling medicine man buried a treasure near Sulphur Springs. Some gold coins that have been found in the area might be part of this treasure.

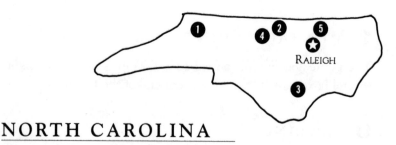

NORTH CAROLINA

❶ ABBOTT CREEK

British general Cornwallis buried the treasure he had stolen from those loyal to the Revolutionary Army and cause on the banks of Abbott Creek. The treasure consisted of gold and silver in chests and kegs. It is buried, according to the legend, a few hundred feet from a bridge on the U.S. 64 highway east of Lexington.

❷ BURLINGTON

As the Civil War wound down, the Confederate treasury was

emptied and the gold buried along the McLeansville to Burlington railroad. Supposedly hundreds of pots filled with treasure were cached along the railroad right of way, all within one hundred paces of the tracks and in groups of three.

❸ CAPE FEAR RIVER

The British pirate, Stede Bonnet, while repairing his ship, went ashore and buried loot from his activities. The three chests contained gold, silver, and jewelry. Before the repairs to the ship could be completed, Stede and his men were surrounded and captured by authorities. Bonnet was later hanged for piracy.

❹ GREENSBORO

William Wentworth buried a sack of gold in the woods between Greensboro and High Point near Brummel's Inn. He died during the night so that relatives were unable to find his treasure.

❺ RUIN CREEK

An old inn and tavern near a place called Ruin Creek was known as the Pop Castle Inn. The owner, a sometime pirate, is supposed to have buried his gold near the tavern. No one has ever found the cache.

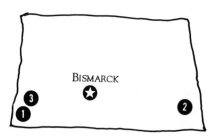

NORTH DAKOTA

❶ FORT DILTS HISTORICAL SITE

A party was split when a wagon overturned. The larger party continued on and, once out of sight, the smaller one was attacked by Sioux. Fearing their gold would be stolen, the men buried it. One man is reported to have carried $40,000 to start a store in Virginia City. The Indians were eventually driven off, but not before the majority of the men were killed, including the man who had hidden the $40,000. The battle site is about thirteen miles from Fort Dilts.

❷ LEONARD

George Trikk stole gold coins from a shipment destined for Fargo. He was chased by a posse and killed near Leonard. The gold was not found with him and it's believed that he buried the money just before he was killed.

❸ SUNSET BUTTE

An Army payroll was sent from Fort Meade in the Black Hills to

Fort Keogh in Montana. When it never arrived, it was assumed that everyone had been ambushed and killed. Around the turn of the century three old pistols and some Army wagon irons were found near Sunset Butte. It is believed this was the lost patrol that buried the gold before they were killed by the Indians.

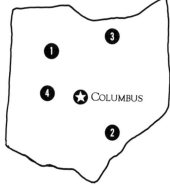

OHIO

❶ FINDLAY

General St. Clair and 2,000 men left an area now known as Cincinnati. Near Findlay, they were attacked by Indians and, fearing that his force would be wiped out, St. Clair buried the payroll gold. St. Clair was wounded and captured by the Indians. He never revealed where the treasure was hidden.

❷ NELSONVILLE

Indians who raided in the area around 1800 used Tinker's Cave as a hideout where it is believed they hid gold and silver.

❸ ROCHESTER

During the French and Indian War, the British attacked Fort Duquesne. A detail of men took sixteen pack animals loaded with gold and silver from the fort to bury it. After the treasure was hidden the detail was attacked by the British. All the men were killed except two who survived and escaped.

The gold was buried in the center of a square formed by four springs. About a half mile from the hole, one of the men forced a rock into the crotch of a tree to mark the spot. Six hundred steps to the north of where the gold was buried, they hid the shovels. About a mile to the east, one of the men carved a deer on a tree.

This area is in Columbiana County on the farm of George Robbins. The rock in the tree and the shovels have been found, but the gold and the rest of the treasure remains hidden.

❹ SPRINGFIELD

John Synder is said to have buried gold coins worth three to four million dollars. It is hidden in land that Synder gave to the city. It is now part of a city park, buried in an area that he called the "abutment."

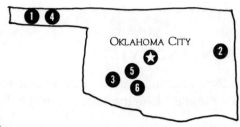

OKLAHOMA

❶ CIMARRON COUNTY

French outlaws heading to New Orleans with gold they had obtained in New Mexico learned that the United States had made the Louisiana Purchase. Afraid that the government would confiscate their gold, estimated value at two and a half million, they buried it in Cimarron County near Sugar Loaf Peak.

❷ Horseshoe Bend

Cherokee Indians hid several urns of gold in a cave in a narrow valley in the Horseshoe Bend area of the Illinois River.

❸ Lawton

Jesse James and his gang buried much of their stolen wealth somewhere along the Cache Creek in Comanche County. Many years afterward, Frank James returned to the area and bought a small farm. Each morning he rode out searching for the treasure they had hidden but he couldn't recognize the territory. There are no reports that anyone found any of the money.

❹ The Panhandle Area

During the Indian Wars, an Army patrol with a payroll of about $42,000 was attacked by Indians. Soldiers buried the money but when the fighting ended, were unable to locate the treasure.

❺ Panther Creek

Dick Estes stole thousands of dollars in jewels and coins in Denver and then headed to the Oklahoma Territory to hide out. He buried everything near Panther Creek on the northern side of the Wichita Mountains in Oklahoma Territory. Estes was then arrested and died in a penitentiary without revealing the location of the loot.

❻ Wichita Mountains

There are stories of a cave with an iron door guarding it. The rumors are that the Spanish used the cave to hide more than eleven million dollars during their exploration of the Southwest. Indian skeletons guard the treasure of gold bars, coins, and silver.

Two people have claimed to have seen the cave, but neither was able to find it again. The treasure, one of the largest, remains hidden.

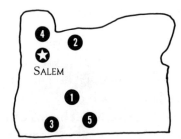

OREGON

❶ Crater Lake

Indians took sixteen mule loads of gold and other valuables from a group of renegades. They threw the gold and dumped the dust in a ravine between the Rogue and Illinois Rivers.

❷ Hood River Valley

A robber built a cabin in the Horse Thief Meadows and hid $25,000 in gold under the floor. When searchers returned, they spent nearly two years looking for the remains of the cabin, and then wasted more time probing for the gold. They left the area empty-handed; rumors are that the gold remains there.

❸ PHOENIX

The paymaster at Fort Grant had a habit of burying, in an iron kettle, the gold and gold dust of various people until he could make the long trip to the bank. He kept at it until he suffered a stroke and could no longer talk. He tried to draw a map so that others could find the hidden treasure but died before he could complete it.

❹ PORTLAND

Three famous gangsters robbed a Portland jewelry store, stealing about $100,000. Afraid they would be captured, they stopped along the old Columbia River highway and buried the loot in two Mason jars. Two of the robbers were later killed in separate shoot-outs with the FBI. The third had remained in the car and didn't know exactly where the jewels had been hidden. He told a friend, but neither man was ever able to recover them.

❺ SWAN LAKE

The gold from several stagecoach robberies is supposed to be buried behind the site of the old post office. Today, no one is sure where the post office stood, so searches for the treasure have failed.

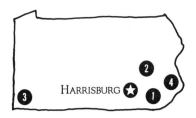

PENNSYLVANIA

❶ DELAWARE WATER GAP

A railroad paymaster, as he became ill, buried the payroll in a copper strong box for safekeeping. He died of a heart attack shortly afterward. A search of the immediate area recovered the key to the box but not the box with the payroll.

❷ MT. CARMEL

An aircraft carrying about a quarter of a million dollars crashed in the area. Before the crash, quite a bit of the cargo was jettisoned, including a package of used bills that weighed about 250 pounds. The wreckage of the plane has been found but the money is still missing.

❸ LAUREL CAVERNS

The Kirk Gang roamed the area in the early nineteenth century and buried a large amount of loot in the cavern.

❹ WASHINGTON'S CROSSING STATE PARK

A man, who was supposed to have been a doctor for Captain Kidd, built a cabin on what is now called Bowman's Hill. Dr. John Bowman, forced into service with Kidd, died in the cabin and his share of the loot from Kidd's raids has never been found.

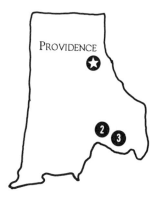

RHODE ISLAND

❶ BLOCK ISLAND

Joseph Bradish apparently used some part of the island to hide a treasure made up of jewels and gold and silver coins. Bradish had sent men to the mainland for provisions, but they were recognized as pirates. Learning that his men were in jail, Bradish scuttled his damaged ship and hid the treasure on the Island. One old reference says, "We buried ye money and ye jewels on the south point of ye island to the leeward."

❷ CONANICUT ISLAND

Several small caches of coins have been found on the one-time residence of Captain Thomas Paine. Rumors are that Paine may have been a pirate and that Captain Kidd's wife once asked him for twenty-four ounces of gold. Paine is said to have returned from a variety of voyages in which he raided ships and buried treasure on the island. Although there are no estimates about the value, it is believed that he raided a large number of English, Spanish, and South American ships and buried gold and silver coins.

❸ NEWPORT

Captain Thomas Tew, a privateer who gave up government protection and turned pirate, eventually retired to the Newport area. According to some estimates, he buried about $100,000. Before he could enjoy it, his former crewman convinced him to make one final raid. He never returned. The treasure is still hidden somewhere near Newport.

SOUTH CAROLINA

❶ CHARLESTON

The owners of the Six Mile Tavern killed and robbed many of their wealthy guests. When a couple of skeletons were discovered in the cellar of the tavern, the locals lynched John and Lavinia Fisher. Many searched for the treasure they believed hidden around the tavern but nothing of importance has been found.

❷ CHESTER

The Confederate government, in the last days of the Civil War, tried to keep their treasury away from the advancing Union Army. The treasure party was finally captured in Georgia but records showed two stops, one near Chester and one near Newberry, where it is possible that the missing $300,000 was hidden.

❸ DARLINGTON

Melvin Purvis, the famous FBI man of the 1930s, retired to the Florence area and became a newspaper publisher. After he died in 1960, many people searched his farm in the Darlington area, looking for treasure that he is rumored to have hidden there.

❹ JAMESTOWN

Confederate gold worth about $200,000 is buried in the vicinity of the Santee River.

More than $63,000 in gold and silver coins were buried on the grounds of the old Hampton House. This site, too, is on the Santee River.

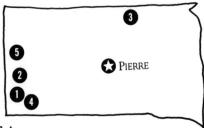

SOUTH DAKOTA

❶ FRENCH CREEK

The traders at Gordon Stockade accumulated gold and silver, probably in violation of various treaties with the local Indians. Learning that the Army was coming to arrest them, the traders took their wealth and escaped. As John Gordon traveled southwest along French Creek, he spotted a cavalry patrol. He buried his gold before crossing the creek, and then headed toward Sioux City, Iowa but died suddenly, before he reached home.

❷ HILL CITY

An old prospector, identified only as Shafer, buried half a washtub of gold near his cabin about two miles outside of Hill City.

❸ LONG LAKE

Gray Foot, a Santee Sioux, told his sons that he had been involved in the destruction of Redwood Agency. After the raid, the Indians found that gold had been delivered to the agency. Gray Foot, like other raiders, helped himself to the gold, putting his share in a flour sack. Later, when he learned that any Santee with gold would be considered one of the murderers, he buried the gold along the lake in Marshall County.

❹ RED CANYON

Joseph Metz buried the small stake his family had collected. Before he could recover it, Indians found them and attacked, killing all of them. The treasure is still where Metz buried it.

❺ SPEARFISH

In 1883, Louis Thoen found a flat rock with a message scratched on it. According to the message, Ezra Kind, along with a number of others, had found gold in the area in 1833. In 1834, they were attacked by Indians and all but Kind were killed. They had taken some of their gold out, but the Indians had stolen all the ponies.

Not far from the stone, the skeleton of a man was found, along with the rusted remains of a gun. It was believed that this was Kind. Hunters found two skeletons northwest of Spearfish. It's believed that they were two of the men mentioned by Kind.

Many have searched for the gold that Kind and his fellows had found, but no one has located anything. The stone found by Thoen is kept in the Adams Memorial Museum in Deadwood.

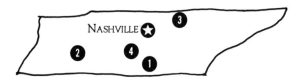

TENNESSEE

❶ COLDWATER

French deserters settled in the Elk River area at the end of the seventeenth century. They apparently formed the first outlaw gang but they also trapped furs. They sold the furs in New Orleans and returned to the Coldwater area with gold and silver. That did them no good simply because there was nowhere to spend the money. They eventually died out, but the rumors persist that they had buried their gold and silver in the area until they could return to France to spend the money.

❷ LEXINGTON

Those fearing the enemy during the Civil War buried more than a million dollars in silver coins, gold, and jewelry somewhere near Owl Creek.

❸ MACON COUNTY

Two miserly brothers named Jones lived their lives together. They never had much money, but sold many crops, converting most of the profits into gold and silver. They didn't trust banks and when they died, within months of one another, their farm was searched but no one found anything. Their gold and silver is still hidden somewhere on their Russell Hill farm.

❹ SOWELL FORD

Farmer Jacob Roaks claimed that he had hidden a number of small treasure caches on his farm near the Sowell Ford on the Duck River. In 1900, two boys were plowing where a corn crib had stood on the Roaks' farm. They found a skillet filled with gold coins. Other such stashes are believed to be hidden in the area.

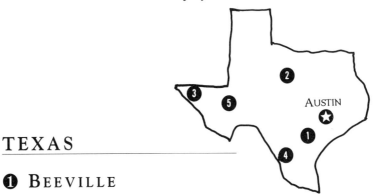

TEXAS

❶ BEEVILLE

A man left his home for San Antonio with $40,000 in gold. He camped one night south of Beeville. When he noticed some riders approaching, he carefully scraped away the coals of his campfire, dug a hole to hide his gold, and covered it over, feeding the fire. He fled from the men who turned out to be bandits. They captured him, dragged him away, and tortured him for several days. He refused to say a word about the gold. When he was released, he tried to find his treasure but was unable to do so.

❷ CLYDE

Midway between Abilene and Cisco is what might be the largest treasure in Texas. Although the information is sketchy and the sources less than reliable, it seems that Coronado might have hidden a treasure worth more than sixty million dollars.

❸ EL PASO

Pancho Villa took a great deal of wealth out of Mexico when he left. Since he didn't trust American banks, he loaded one of his touring cars and drove up into the Franklin Mountains. There he buried a treasure of undetermined size in a hidden cave. On a rock near the entrance, they carved the word *oro*.

❹ ESPANTOSA LAKE

A wagon train loaded with gold and silver camped by the side of the lake. Fearing an attack by Indians, they buried their treasure. Early the next morning the Indians did attack and all the men were killed. Two women were captured and held for several years. They were finally released and one of the women tried to lead a party back to the site of the battle but she was unable to find it.

❺ SIMBERLY

After the Civil War, a ranchhand, L.J. Dailey, was hunting with friends. As he climbed a hill, he grabbed a rock and it broke loose in his hand. Because it seemed uncommonly heavy, he put it in his pocket. When he examined it later, he saw that it was very rich silver ore. Although he tried to retrace his steps, he was unable to find the ledge.

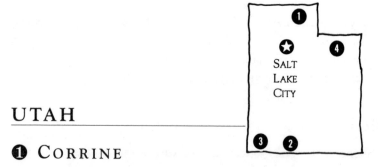

UTAH

❶ CORRINE

Three men, Jack Wright, George H. Tipton, and George Witherell, robbed a train just south of Colorado Springs, getting away with $105,000 in cash and $40,000 in jewels. They were pursued by a posse but escaped, working their way through Colorado to Wyoming and then on into Idaho. Eventually, following the Bear River, they ended up near Corrine, in a spot known as Box Elder Canyon. They buried the majority of treasure, keeping out small amounts of cash and jewelry.

One of the men found himself in a card game in Corrine and put up a watch taken in the robbery as a bet. He lost, and the watch was identified as having come from the train robbery. Wright and Witherell were arrested, but Tipton escaped, wounded in the attempt.

He managed to reach the ranch of Laf Roberts who tried to help him. Tipton died on the ranch, but not before he told Roberts about the treasure. Tipton drew a crude map and Roberts was able to find some of the landmarks. Warned that he would be arrested if he found any of the treasure, Roberts gave up the search. There are no indications that much of the loot was ever recovered.

❷ Kanab

It has been reported that ten million dollars in gold and silver was stolen from the Aztec Empire in the sixteenth century by Spanish explorers. The treasure is hidden in the caves of White Mountain.

❸ St. George

Brigham Young buried a number of caches of gold coins around St. George. Three different finds were discovered in 1963 and 1964, but it is rumored that additional caches remain hidden in the area.

❹ Unitah Mountains

Spanish explorers are said to have found and worked a rich gold deposit near a point where two streams come together in a remote canyon. The treasure is hidden by the mine and guarded by skeletons.

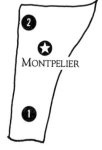

MONTPELIER

VERMONT

❶ Bellows Falls

Captain Kidd supposedly buried a treasure in the area. In 1839, workmen digging a canal found a small cache of silver coins, pieces-of-eight, and silver ingots.

❷ St. Albans

Civil War records show that a group of Rebels raided the town on October 19, 1864. They robbed the three banks, stealing about $200,000. They shot their way out of town, killing one man and wounding four others. A posse was formed, chasing the Rebels to the Canadian border. That didn't stop either the Rebels or the posse.

The Rebels were finally captured in Canada and turned over to the Canadian authorities. Only $75,000 was recovered. Later, one of the soldiers said that they had buried the gold because it was heavy and slowing them down. It was somewhere between the town and the border in a pine grove along the trail. There were seven canvas bags containing about $120,000.

It should be noted that the Rebels were released in December 1864, because of a technicality. There is no indication that any of them returned to recover the treasure.

❸ STAVE ISLAND

This is just a rumor of treasure based on faith in the story, not unlike the faith in the Oak Island treasure. A laborer who was eating his lunch noticed a hand with an extended, pointing finger, carved on the side of a tree. At first he paid no attention, but then began wondering about it. He climbed the tree, sighted along the finger, and saw that it pointed to a rock. He climbed down and found the rock, but couldn't budge it himself.

A day or two later, he returned with a friend. However, the caretaker of the island, suspecting they were hunting treasure, told them that any loot found would have to be surrendered to the owner of the island. The caretaker eventually changed his mind, telling the laborer that he would help in the search if he could share in the treasure.

For some reason, they didn't get back to the island quickly. A forest fire burned all the trees, so the clue to the rock was lost. No one else ever suggested that anything of value was hidden on the island.

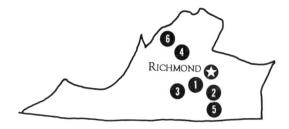

VIRGINIA

❶ CUMBERLAND GAP

Not long after Daniel Boone carved the Wilderness Road through the mountains, one man built a tavern and roadhouse. It has been rumored that the owner worked a gold mine, but because of the great distance to the nearest banks, stockpiled the treasure, burying it near his tavern. He was killed by Indians. Searches of the area near Ewing have failed to find the treasure.

❷ HOPEWELL

A rich farmer named Cousins buried three half-gallon sized fruit jars filled with gold and silver coins just after the stock market crash of 1929. He was killed in an accident before he recovered the treasure, or told his family exactly where he had hidden it.

❸ LYNCHBURG

There is very good evidence that various families living in the area hid their family fortunes during the Civil War. Gold and silver coins, jewels, and various other valuables totaling as much as two million dollars were buried. Many of the caches have not been recovered.

➍ NEW BALTIMORE

During the Civil War, John Mosby and his raiders captured Union General Edwin H. Stoughton who had about $350,000 in stolen gold, silver, and other valuables in his possession. Mosby and one of his sergeants buried the treasure between Haymarket and New Baltimore. The sergeant was later captured and hanged. Mosby had intended to return to recover the treasure, but was prevented by the fortunes of war. Mosby later disbanded his unit and it wasn't until he was dying in 1916 that he mentioned the treasure and location to anyone.

➎ PETERSBURG

Many of the people living in the area during the Civil War seige buried their gold, silver, and jewels to keep them from being taken by the Union forces.

➏ WINCHESTER

Three slaves owned by Dr. Berkley murdered him and stole his bag of gold coins. Afraid they would be caught with the bag, the men buried it near the slave quarters. A few days later they were hung without telling where the money had been hidden. Berkley's family never found it.

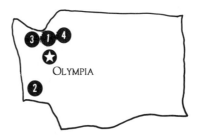

WASHINGTON

❶ COMMENCEMENT BAY

In 1894, after days of heavy rain, the hillsides around Commencement Bay gave way. The mudslide carried away buildings and destroyed some of the docks. A safe belonging to the Northern Pacific Railway was buried in the mud. It contained $2,400 in cash and $1,200 in gold coins. The treasure would be worth considerably more in today's market.

❷ FORT COLUMBIA MILITARY RESERVATION

Captain John Scarborough built his house near what is now Battery No. 2. During his life, he accumulated a fortune in small gold bars, which he buried in a small keg near his house. Although Scarborough's wife supposedly knew the location, she never recovered the gold. Scarborough's son, Ned, spent his life searching for the treasure.

❸ PORT ANGELES

A customs agent, Victor Smith, had a strongbox containing about $1,500 in cash and $7,500 in gold coins when a flood struck. The strongbox disappeared. Later it was reported that Indians had taken and buried it near their village close to Port Angeles. Though one of the Indians was arrested, the site of the treasure was never disclosed.

❹ Vashon Island

Les Hanson was a lumberman who had a good business in the area. He married a local Indian who was afraid of robbers and hid her money in a number of small caches to defeat the thieves. She was killed shortly after, before she could tell Hanson where the gold coins were hidden.

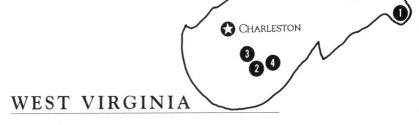

CHARLESTON

WEST VIRGINIA

❶ Charles Town

During the Indian Wars at the end of the eighteenth century, several of the residents of the area buried their personal treasures, gold and silver coins, and jewels, near the St. George Chapel. For some reason, the Indians did not attack or burn the Chapel. Many of these small treasures were not recovered.

❷ Denmar

Ed and Ike Colter lived on a farm in the area. They didn't believe in banks, so they buried their gold. Ike Colter told a friend that he had buried quite a bit. Ed was shot and Ike was blamed but Ike's guilt was never proven. Only the chimney of the house remains but it is an easily found landmark.

❸ GAULEY BRIDGE

The bridge where the Gauley and New Rivers form the Great Kanawha River is one site where treasure was buried a number of times. One rumored treasure was buried by the Confederate Army near the bridge during the Civil War. Other stories persist that other treasures were buried near the bridge as well.

❹ MARLINGTON

Three Italian men killed their fellow railroad workers, taking all their combined savings. The loot was then split among the three. One of the men decided that he would bury his share of the gold, selecting a V-shaped field along the Greenbriar River about two miles from Marlington. At the river's edge was a stone cliff with a number of flat rocks at the base of the cliff. The gold was hidden under one of these rocks. Shortly after he buried the gold, he was captured and died in the electric chair for his part in the murders.

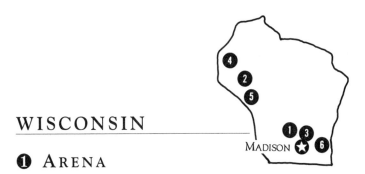

WISCONSIN

❶ ARENA

Two Indians stole gold from a riverboat in the ealy 1880s. They escaped to the east and hid the treasure in a cave on the Coon Rock Bluff. They were chased by a posse and killed while being arrested.

❷ IRVINGTON

A group of French soldiers were moving through the area, along the Red Cedar River. When they spotted a large party of Indians, they buried some of the heavier equipment and a great deal of gold. Some people claim it is hidden in a cave near Pinnacle.

❸ MADISON

A party of soldiers was carrying a chest of gold from Fort Dearborn in Chicago to Fort Crawford in Prairie du Chien. Chased by a war party that was closing in on them, they dropped the chest through a hole in the ice of Lake Mandota. They escaped but were unable to recover the chest.

❹ Osceola

William Snow and several others were caught by a group of French and Indians. Snow was carrying a large quantity of English gold coins, which he buried before the French attacked. The story is that he buried the money among the wooden bluffs on the river banks west of the city.

❺ Pepin County

An Army courier carrying gold was chased by Indians. He hid the gold and then galloped off, eluding his pursuers. When he came back, he couldn't locate the missing treasure.

❻ West Allis

Road crews building a freeway found just under $8,000 in cash. Mrs. Thomas Burke claimed the money due to the fact that it had been on property she had owned before the government had condemned the land. She said that another $8,000 to $10,000 was buried in glass jars in the area.

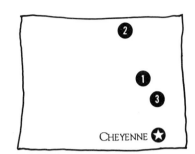

WYOMING

❶ CONVERSE COUNTY

Robbers stole an Army patrol and were quickly tracked down by soldiers. In the gun battle that followed all were killed or badly wounded. Before the last of the robbers died, he said they had hidden the $40,000 in a cave on Deer Creek.

❷ SHERIDAN

After the Fetterman massacre in December 1866, the remaining officers at Fort Phil Kearny believed the Sioux were about to attack. Colonel Carrington, the commanding officer, ordered the paymaster to bury gold coins in two chests so that the money wouldn't fall into the hands of the Indians. The Sioux, however, retreated into winter quarters and there was no attack. One of the chests was recovered by the Army, but the other remains buried.

❸ SLADE CANYON

Joseph A. Slade, who had a job as superintendent of the Overland Stage Line, was also a bandit leader. The gang robbed wagon trains and buried the loot in Slade Canyon. Slade was eventually arrested and hung in Montana for shooting up a general store.

BIBLIOGRAPHY

—

ANDERSON, EUGENE. "Ben Sublett's Lost Mine: Did it Ever Exist?" *True West* (September/October 1970): 23–27.

_____. "Hidden Gold of the Guadalupes." *True Treasure* (January/February 1972): 28–31.

BALLINGER, GENE. "The Mystery People." *The (Hatch, NM) Courier* (January 28, 1993): 1, 3–4.

_____. "Ogam Alphabet Found, Deciphered, Near Victorio Peak." *The (Hatch, NM) Courier* (March 4, 1993): 1–2, 9.

_____. "Victorio Peak: No Longer An Enigma." *The (Hatch, NM) Courier* (August 27, 1992): 1–2, 5–6, 9, 11.

"Believes Rich Mine Covered Up By Indians." *El Paso Herald* (August 13, 1927).

BRYAN, HOWARD. "The White Sands' Doc Noss Treasure Story May Not Be Myth After All." *El Paso Herald Post*, October 20, 1973.

_____. "Mrs. Noss Tells Her Story of Discovery." *El Paso Herald Post*, October 21, 1973.

CARSON, KIT. "Lost Ben Sublett Mine." *True Treasure* (January/February 1970): 30–36.

CARSON, XANTHUS. "The Incredible Victorio Peak Treasure." *True Treasure* (November/December 1968): 11–21.

CHANDLER, DAVID. "The Mysterious Treasure of Victorio Peak." *Rolling Stone* (December 18, 1975).

CONNELL, EVAN S. *Son of the Morning Star*. San Francisco: North Point Press, 1984.

CORBIN, HELEN. *Senner's Gold*. Phoenix, AR: Foxwest Publishing, 1993.

DALEY, ROBERT. *Treasure*. New York: Random House, 1977.

DAVID, LESTER. "The Secret of the Money Pit." *Boy's Life* (September 1992): 32.

DOBIE, JAMES FRANK. *Legends of Texas*. Dallas: SMU Press, 1976.

———. *Lost Mines and Buried Treasures*. New York: Grosset and Dunlap, 1930.

DRAGO, HARRY SINCLAIR. *Lost Bonanzas*. New York: Dodd, Mead & Co., 1966.

EBERHART, PERRY. *Treasure Tales of the Rockies*. Athens: Swallow Press, 1969.

ECKLES, JIM. "The Victorio Peak Story." *Missile Ranger (White Sands Missile Range Newspaper)* (January 26, 1990; February 9, 1990; February 16, 1990; February 23, 1990; March 2, 1990; July 20, 1990; November 2, 1990; and March 12, 1990).

"El Pasoan Guides Two Parties In Search for Supposedly Rich Lost Adams Diggin's." *El Paso Herald* (January 14, 1926).

"El Pasoan Learns Story of Famous Lost Diggin's From Adams's Partner." *El Paso Herald* (December 24, 1927).

"El Pasoan Tells How He Got Map To Hidden Placer." *El Paso Herald* (August 6, 1927): 9.

"Following the Will o' Wisp, 'The Lost Adams Diggin's.'" *El Paso Herald* (July 2, 1927): 10.

FREEMAN, PATRICIA and MATHISON, DIRK. "Writer D'Arcy O'Connor, Digging Deep Into 'Money Pit' Lore, Unearths a Trove of Mysteries." *People* (March 6, 1989): 235.

FROST, LAWRENCE. *Custer Legends*. Ohio: Bowling Green University, 1981.

FURNEAUX, RUPERT. *The Money Pit Mystery*. New York: Dodd, Mead & Co. 1972.

GARCIA, GUY and HAEDERLE. "In Search of a Legend: Doc Noss' Treasure Was Vast, But Did It Really Exist?" *People* (September 14, 1992): 137.

GODWIN, JOHN. *This Baffling World*. New York: Hart Publishing, Co., Inc., 1968.

GRONEMAN, BILL. *Defense of a Legend*. Plano, TX: Wordware Publishing, 1994.

HENSON, MICHAEL PAUL. *America's Lost Treasures*. South Bend, IN: Jayco Publishing Co., 1984.

_____. *A Guide to Treasure in Pennsylvania*. Deming, NM: Carson Enterprises, 1981.

_____. *Guide to Treasure in Tennessee*. Deming, NM: Carson Enterprises, 1987.

HULT, RUBY E. *Lost Mines and Treasures*. Portland, OR: Binfords & Mort, 1960.

HUNTER, J. MARVIN. "Mysterious Gold Mine of the Guadalupe Mountains." *Hunter's Frontier Magazine* (October 1916): 177–179.

"Indians Befriend Survivor Of Massacre of Party Which Located Adams Diggin's." *El Paso Herald* (January 7, 1928).

JAMESON, W. C. *Buried Treasures of the American Southwest*. Little Rock, AR: August House, Inc., 1989.

_____. *Buried Treasures of the Rocky Mountain West*. Little Rock, AR: August House, 1993.

_____. *Buried Treasures of Texas*. Little Rock, AR: August House, Inc., 1989.

KENNEDY, B. F. *Buried Treasure of Casco Bay*. New York: Vantage Press, 1963.

KOURY, PHIL A. *Treasure of Victoria Peak*. West Chester, PA: Schiffer Publishing Ltd., 1981.

LAIRD, CHARLTON GRANT. *Iowa Legends of Buried Treasure*. Lincoln, NE: Foundation Books, 1990.

LASCO, JACK. "Captain Kidd's Buried $21 Million." *SAGA'S Treasure Special 1975* (1975): 8.

_____. "Gulf Coast Gold Rush for Jean Lafitte's Missing Millions." *SAGA's Treasure Special 1975* (1975): 20.

"The Lost Adams Diggin's Are Still Lost." *El Paso Herald Post* (September 21, 1937).

"The Lost Adams Diggings." *Colorado*. (March/April 1972): 24–32.

"A Lost Mine Richer Than Solomon's or the Klondike." *El Paso Herald* (February 16, 1916).

"Massacre Of Prospectors Who Found Adams Diggin's Told By Eye Witness." *El Paso Herald* (December 31, 1927).

MASTERS, AL. "The Complete Story of the Beale Treasure Codes." *SAGA's Special 1976 Treasure* (1976): 8.

MCDONALD, DOUGLAS. *Nevada Lost Mines and Buried Treasures*. Las Vegas, NV: Nevada Publications, 1981.

MITCHELL, JOHN D. *Lost Mines and Buried Treasures Along the Old Frontier*. Glorieta, NM: The Rio Grande Press, Inc., 1987.

NESMITY, ROBERT I. *Dig for Pirate Treasure*. New York: The Devin-Adair Co., 1958.

O'CONNOR, D'ARCY. *The Big Dig: The $10 Million Search for Oak Island's Legendary Treasure*. New York: Ballantine Books, 1988.

PAINE, RALPH D. *The Book of Buried Treasure*. New York: Arno Press, 1981.

PENFIELD, THOMAS. *Buried Treasure in the U.S. and Where to Find It*. New York: Tempo Books, 1954.

_____. *Directory of Buried or Sunken Treasures and Lost Mines of the United States*. Conroe, TX: True Treasure Library, 1971.

PEPPER, CHORAL. *Treasure Legends of the West*. Salt Lake City, UT: Gibbs-Smith Publisher, 1994.

POAG, THOMASINE. "The Legendary Cache of Red Bone Cave." *SAGA's Special 1976 Treasure* (1976): 38.

PRESTON, DOUGLAS. "Death Trap Defies Treasure Seekers for Two Centuries." *Smithsonian* (June 1988): 62–63.

"Prospector Spends 40 Yrs. Hunting Lost Adams." *El Paso Herald* (August 13, 1927).

QUARRELL, CHARLES. *Buried Treasure*. London: MacDonald & Evans, Ltd., 1955.

"Renegade Indians and White Outlaws Are Guarding Placer Even Today, Hudson Believes." *El Paso Herald* (January 16, 1927): 10.

"The Secret of Oak Island." *National Geographic World* (June 1989): 22.

SIKORSKY, ROBERT. *Quest for the Dutchman's Gold*. Phoenix, AR: Golden West Publishers, 1983.

"Story of Lost Gold Strike Recalled as Prospectors Again Seek 'Adams Diggin's.'" *El Paso Herald-Post* (October 18, 1932).

SWANSON, JAMES A. and KOLLENBORN, THOMAS J. *Circlestone: A Superstitition Mountain Mystery*. Apache Junction, AR: Goldfield Press, 1986.

TERRY, THOMAS P. *Missing Mobster Millions and Other Gangland Gold*. La Cross, WI: Specialty Publishing Co., 1980.

VERRILL, ALPHEUS HYATT. *Lost Treasure: True Tales of Hidden Hoards.* New York: D. Appleton and Co., 1930.

WILKINS, HAROLD T. *Captain Kidd and His Skeleton Island.* New York: Liveright Publishing Corp., 1937.

WINTERS, WAYNE. *Forgotten Mines and Treasures.* Tombstone, AR: Tombstone Nuget Publishing, Co., 1972.

PERIODICALS

Gold and Treasure Hunter, PO Box 47, Happy Camp, CA 96039.

Lost Treasure, PO Box 1589, Grove, OK 74344.

Treasure Search, Lone Eagle Productions, 33065 Yucaipa Blvd., Yucaipa, CA 92399.

Western & Eastern Treasures, PO Box 1598, Mercer Island, WA 98040.

SAGA's Treasure Special